1000+ Fun, Interesting And Mind-Blowing Facts For Curious Minds.

DAVE QUILLON

Table of Contents

INTRODUCTION

Hello, young explorers and inquisitive minds! Are you ready to dive into a treasure trove of wonders with "1001 Fun and Mind-blowing Facts For Curious Hearts "? Imagine a journey where each turn of the page whisks you away to an exhilarating new realm—be it the mysterious depths of the ocean, the twinkling reaches of outer space, or the hidden corners of ancient history! This isn't just any book; it's a magical passport to a universe where learning sparkles with fun, and every single fact is a step on an exciting adventure.

We'll meet creatures with amazing secrets, inventors who dreamed the impossible, and brave heroes from tales old and new. Our quest for knowledge will take us through the jungles of the wild, into the labs of mad scientists, and across time to lands where dinosaurs still roam and castles keep their stories stone silent. If you've ever wondered about the stars above or the earth below, this is the perfect guide for your ever-curious heart.

Get ready to saddle up your imagination and set off on a learning spree where every fact is a playdate with wonder, and every moment spent reading is as thrilling as discovering a hidden superpower. Welcome aboard, dear reader—let the amazement begin!

WHY ARE FUN FACTS IMPORTANT FOR KIDS?

1. **Fun facts are like treasure for your brain**: Just like pirates find treasures, fun facts are exciting treasures for your mind! When you learn something new and fun, like how a cat has five toes on its front paws but only four toes on the back, it sticks in your brain. Remembering fun facts is easier because they surprise you and make you say "Wow!" And when learning is fun, you just want to keep doing it.

2. **Share the fun and watch friendships grow**: Imagine you're sharing a bag of your favorite snacks with a friend. Sharing fun facts is similar, but what you share won't finish; it just gets bigger! When you tell your friends that butterflies taste with their feet, you'll have their attention in no time. It's a cool way to break the ice and start chatting, turning playtime into a fun learning session, too!

3. **Becoming a little explorer of knowledge**: Every time you learn a fun fact, think of it as getting a key to a new door. Behind it, there's a whole new world to explore! For example, if you learn that stars can be different colors based on how hot they are, you might start looking at the night sky more and asking questions like an astronaut on a space mission. It's

a way to build up your brain muscles, making you smarter and giving you the confidence to ask more questions and find more answers on your own.

HOW TO USE THIS BOOK

This book is full of cool stuff to learn and share. Here's how to use it:

👪 **Read Together:** Sit with someone and take turns reading the facts out loud. It's a fun way to spend time together and learn cool things.

🔍 **Look Things Up:** When you're curious about something, find it in this book and learn more about it. It's like a treasure hunt for your brain!

🎯 **Play Fact Games:** Use the facts to play guessing games or have a quiz night with friends. It makes learning a blast and helps you remember better.

Take this book on a nature walk or look for stuff around your house that's in the book. It's a great way to see and do new things!

💡 **Find Out More:** If you read a fact that's super interesting, look up more about it. Share what you find with family and friends—it'll make you super smart!

Have fun using this book to explore and learn every day! 🌈

ENVIRONMENT, NATURE, PLANT & ANIMALS

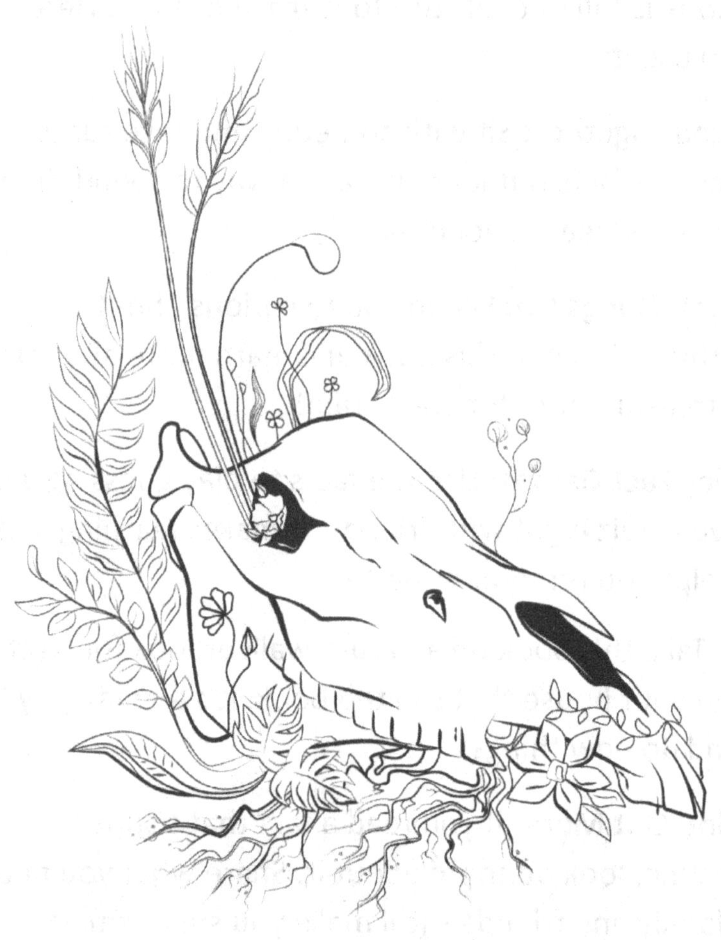

1. The Amazon Rainforest, often called the "lungs of the Earth," produces more than 20% of the world's oxygen supply.

2. The "Midnight Sun" phenomenon above the Arctic Circle results in 24 hours of sunlight for several weeks, usually from late May to late July.

3. Cats have an average lifespan of 14 years, although some can live into their 20s. In fact, it is not uncommon for cats to reach the grand old age of 20. To calculate a cat's life in human years is not as straightforward as most people believe. The first cat year is 15 years, the second cat year is 9. This makes a cat 24 at the age of two! Then it's a simple case of adding 4 years for every human year. If a cat lives for 20 years, it is 96 in equivalent human years!

4. Mawsynram in India, has the world's wettest climate on Earth. It receives over 460 inches of rain every year!

5. The durian fruit, often referred to as the "king of fruits" in Southeast Asia, has a notorious smell that some people find pleasant and sweet, while others find it repulsive and nauseating. In fact, the smell is so strong that durians are banned from many hotels and public transportation systems in the region. I've actually tried it. It's really not quite as bad as everyone makes out!

6. Stonefish are some of the most venomous fish in the world, with potent neurotoxins in their spines. They are also masters of camouflage, blending seamlessly with their surroundings on the ocean floor. Interestingly, stonefish can survive out of water for up to 24 hours.

7. In Kuching, Malaysia, you'll find a city that embraces its feline residents. Kuching translates to "cat" in Malay, and the city has numerous cat statues, a cat museum, and even a cat-themed café. It's the purr-fect destination for cat lovers.

8. Vampire bats are the only mammals that feed exclusively on blood. While their diet may seem creepy, they're actually quite beneficial to their ecosystems, as they help control insect populations. Plus, vampire bats are incredibly social animals that engage in cooperative behaviors, like sharing food with their roost-mates.

9. Unicorn horns, also known as "alicorns," were once believed to have magical properties and were highly valued during the Middle Ages and the Renaissance. They were thought to neutralize poison, cure various illnesses, and purify water. In reality, many of the so-called "unicorn horns" were actually narwhal tusks, which were traded at high prices in European markets and did none of these things.

10. The male water shrew, a small insectivorous mammal, has venomous saliva that it uses to paralyze its prey. Interestingly, only the males possess this venomous trait, while the females are completely harmless.

11. Lake Hillier in Western Australia is naturally bright pink due to the presence of a specific type of algae and bacteria that produce pigments under certain

conditions. Despite its unusual color, the water is completely safe for humans to swim in.

12. Komodo dragons are the world's largest lizards, and they have a fearsome reputation for their powerful bite. It was once believed that their bite was venomous, but it's actually their saliva teeming with harmful bacteria that can cause serious infections.

13. Scorpions are often feared for their venomous stings, but they have an interesting quirk that few people know about. Under ultraviolet light, scorpions glow a bright blue-green color. Scientists are still unsure of the exact purpose of this fluorescence.

14. Toucans have the super cool ability to regulate their body temperature just by changing the blood flow in their beaks!

15. Honey badgers have a reputation for being fearless and aggressive animals. However, their boldness is mainly due to their thick skin, which protects them from bites and stings. Despite their tough exterior, honey badgers have a sweet tooth and often raid beehives to enjoy honey, just like their name suggests.

16. Spiny lobsters, unlike their clawed cousins, have no claws to defend themselves. Instead, they have a unique method of protection: they rub their antennae together to produce a loud, raspy noise that can scare away predators.

17. Bats are the only mammal species capable of true, sustained flight. Unlike gliding mammals, such as flying squirrels, bats have elongated fingers and a thin membrane of skin called the patagium, which allows them to actively fly and maneuver through the air.

18. Giraffes are not only known for their towering height, but also for their extraordinary hearts! These gentle giants have hearts that pump twice as hard as a cow's heart to ensure that blood reaches their brains, which are quite a distance away!

19. In the wild, only one in every 10,000 oysters produces a pearl, making these stunning gems an exceptional find!

20. Some of the world's finest hard cheeses, such as Cheddar and Gruyere, are aged in natural caves with specific temperature and humidity conditions. These caves provide a unique environment that fosters the growth of beneficial bacteria and mold!

21. Let's debunk the popular myth about lemmings—these cute little rodents do not commit mass suicide by jumping off cliffs! This widespread misconception has been perpetuated by various media sources, but in reality, lemmings are just as keen on survival as any other creature.

22. Despite their graceful appearance, giraffes can be quite dangerous when they feel threatened. They have powerful legs that can deliver a kick strong enough to kill a lion.

23. Some spiders, like the diving bell spider, can live underwater by creating air bubbles they carry with them like tiny scuba tanks. They spin a dome-shaped web to catch their prey and use the trapped air bubble to breathe.

24. Cats have a keen sense of smell. They have a specialised organ called the Jacobson's organ in the roof of their mouths that allows them to detect pheromones and other scents.

25. We all know that Pufferfish are the masters of self-defense. When faced with danger, they can inflate their bodies to appear larger and less appetizing to predators. However, their real claim to fame is their artistic ability. Male pufferfish create intricate, symmetrical patterns in the sand to attract females, proving that even dangerous animals can have a creative side!

26. Platypuses are not only one of the few venomous mammals, but they also lay eggs, making them one of the most unusual creatures on the planet. What's more, they use electroreceptors in their bills to detect prey hidden in the mud.

27. Tomatoes, eggplants, potatoes, and peppers share a family connection—they're all part of the nightshade family of plants! Despite their diverse appearances and flavors, these culinary favorites have a botanical bond that unites them in the plant world. Tobacco, and of course deadly nightshade, is also a member of the same family!

28. The castor oil plant contains a chemical that is 6,000 times more deadly than cyanide, despite its common name.

29. The African crested rat has a unique method of self-defense—it chews on the bark of a toxic tree and then applies the poisonous saliva to specialized hairs on its back. When a predator bites the rat, it gets a mouthful of deadly toxins. Talk about a surprising and creative survival tactic!

30. The bottom and upper teeth of a crocodile are always on display, even when they shut their mouths.

31. The mantis shrimp can punch with the speed of a bullet, accelerating at over 10,000 times the force of gravity. Its strike is so powerful that it can break aquarium glass and even create small shockwaves underwater.

32. The brain of a cockroach is located inside its body, not its head. If a cockroach loses its head, it can still survive for several weeks, ultimately succumbing to dehydration or starvation.

33. The mimic octopus is known for its incredible ability to imitate the appearance and behavior of other marine animals. This clever cephalopod can impersonate everything from a venomous lionfish to a poisonous sea snake, effectively deterring would-be predators.

34. Hyenas are known for their distinctive "laugh," which is actually a vocalization used to communicate

with one another. Contrary to popular belief, they're not just laughing at their prey!

35. Grapefruits grow in clusters on their trees, resembling the way grapes grow on a vine. That's why they're called grapefruits!

36. Some species of frogs can survive being frozen solid. When temperatures drop, certain frogs, like the wood frog, can enter a state of suspended animation, during which their heart stops beating and their body effectively freezes. As temperatures rise, the frogs thaw out and resume normal function!

37. Swans are often associated with elegance and beauty, but they can be surprisingly aggressive when defending their territory or offspring. With their strong wings and sharp beaks, swans are capable of inflicting painful injuries. Even the most graceful creatures can have a feisty side!

38. Although sharks are often depicted as ferocious predators, humans are more likely to be bitten by other people than by sharks. In fact, you have a higher chance of being struck by lightning or attacked by a cow than being bitten by a shark!

39. A single bolt of lightning contains enough energy to toast approximately 100,000 slices of bread.

40. Saluki dogs, one of the oldest known dog breeds, were originally bred in ancient Egypt as hunting companions for royalty.

41. It is said that the blue whale's heart is so large that a human could actually swim through its arteries!

42. The Clark's nutcracker, a bird native to North America, can remember the locations of thousands of seeds it has hidden throughout its territory.

43. Historians are of the opinion that Genghis Khan was responsible for the establishment of one of the world's first international postal systems.

44. The Indo-Pacific Sailfish is thought to be the species of fish that can swim the quickest.

45. The African bush elephant is the largest living animal that lives on land.

46. China is home to the world's largest population of giant pandas.

47. Mosquitoes are responsible for spreading diseases like malaria and dengue fever, making them one of the most dangerous animals in the world.

48. The dingo, often known as a wild dog, is found exclusively in Australia.

49. Charles Goodyear invented vulcanized rubber when he accidentally dropped a combination of rubber and sulfur on his stove.

50. Ancient Egyptians were such devoted cat lovers that they would shave off their eyebrows to express their grief over the death of their feline companions.

51. The cuckoo bird is notorious for laying its eggs in other birds' nests.

52. The world's largest playable instrument is the Great Stalacpipe Organ, located in Luray Caverns, Virginia.

53. Bamboo holds the title for the fastest-growing plant on Earth, with some species capable of skyrocketing up to 35 inches per day.

54. The mantis shrimp has one of the most complex eyes in the animal kingdom, allowing it to see colours that humans cannot even imagine.

55. The Venus flytrap, a carnivorous plant, can digest an insect in about 10 days.

56. A newborn kangaroo, called a joey, is only about 1 inch long when born and must crawl into its mother's pouch to continue developing.

57. The axolotl, a type of salamander, has the incredible ability to regenerate lost limbs, heart, and even parts of its brain.

58. The Carolina Reaper holds the title for the world's hottest pepper. They are about 200 times hotter than a jalapeno pepper!

59. A medium-sized cumulus cloud weighs about the same as 100 elephants.

60. The Amazon rainforest, often called the "lungs of the Earth," boasts a staggering 400 billion individual trees spanning more than 16,000 species.

61. Pineapples don't grow on trees. They are actually a type of bromeliad, a plant that grows close to the ground and forms a rosette of leaves with the fruit in the centre.

62. The smell of freshly cut grass is actually a distress signal. When grass is cut or injured, it releases volatile organic compounds called green leaf

volatiles (GLVs), which help to seal the wound and prevent infection. The scent produced by GLVs is what we perceive as the fresh-cut grass smell.

63. When crows come together, they form a group known as a "murder."

64. The purr of a cat can vary in pitch and volume, with some producing a high-pitched sound and others a low rumble.

65. In many cultures, it's considered unfortunate to see a black cat. Black cats have long been linked to witchcraft and the supernatural.

66. Hippopotamuses are notoriously hostile. If you ever encounter a hippo, be sure to keep far away.

67. The Titan arum, affectionately dubbed the "corpse flower", is one of the world's largest and most pungent blooms.

68. The world's oldest known living tree is a Great Basin Bristlecone pine named Methuselah.

69. Sloths are such slow movers that algae can grow on their fur, providing them with a form of camouflage in their natural habitat.

70. The world's smallest flowering plant is the Wolffia, or watermeal.

71. The red "hourglass" marking on the underside of the black widow spider is not always an hourglass shape.

72. The Antarctic blue whale is the world's biggest mammal, weighing up to 200 tonnes.

73. Except for Antarctica, spiders can be found on every continent.

74. Flamingos are often observed standing on one leg for extended periods of time. This is supposed to aid in body heat conservation.

75. The human body reacts quickly and in a variety of different ways in response to changing environmental conditions, including temperature and humidity. For example, our bodies adapt in order to ensure that our cells continue to receive the necessary amount of oxygen when we travel to high elevations!

76. Due to its location in a deep valley, the Italian town of Viganella experiences complete darkness during the winter months.

77. The Atacama Desert in Chile is considered the driest non-polar desert on Earth, with some parts receiving less than 1 mm of rainfall annually.

78. Vending machines kill more people than sharks: On average, vending machines are responsible for two to three deaths per year, while sharks cause about one death annually.

79. While Mount Everest is the tallest mountain above sea level, Mauna Kea in Hawaii is actually the tallest when measured from its base on the ocean floor.

80. Bir Tawil, a small area of land between Egypt and Sudan, is one of the few places on Earth that remains unclaimed by any country.

81. Despite being a small country, the Netherlands has the highest concentration of museums per square mile in the world.

82. There's a tiny island called Vulcan Point within Crater Lake, which is itself situated on an island called Taal Volcano Islands in the Philippines. This geological oddity is nestled within Lake Taal, which is on the main island of Luzon!

83. Mars has two moons called Phobos and Deimos. At one time, it was thought that these two moons were captured asteroids. However, in the case of the moons of Mars, it is now believed they are what remains from a giant impact on the planet.

84. The Sun has a strong magnetic field that causes sunspots and solar flares, which can have an effect on Earth's atmosphere and communication systems. The Sun has an 11-year sunspot cycle.

85. The Sahara Desert, the world's largest hot desert, was once a lush, green landscape approximately 10,000 years ago, with evidence of lakes, rivers, and diverse animal life.

86. A wild boar is capable of reaching a top speed of up to 25 miles per hour when running.

87. True nuts include things like hazelnuts, chestnuts, and acorns. Walnuts, pecans, and almonds are not true nuts but rather the seeds of drupes which have a soft fruit around a hard pit containing a seed.

88. Spiders predate the age of the dinosaurs. Fossils of insects that resemble spiders have been discovered that date back to the Devonian era, which occurred more than 400 million years ago.

89. Swiss cheese develops holes because of the carbon dioxide gas created by microorganisms in the milk.

90. There are more than 32,000 distinct fish species found around the world!

91. In addition to having the largest Muslim population, India also has the largest Hindu population.

92. More than ten thousand distinct species of ants can be found worldwide.

93. The 43-foot tall Cuexcomate volcano, located in Mexico, is often mistakenly referred to as the "world's smallest volcano". It is actually a geyser!

94. The "immortal jellyfish" has the unique ability to revert to its juvenile form after reaching maturity. This process can theoretically continue indefinitely, making the immortal jellyfish a fascinating example of nature's ability to cheat death!

95. The Black Mamba is one of the deadliest snakes in the world. These snakes grow up to 14 feet long and they are famed for their speed and agility. If you're ever fortunate (or should that be unfortunate) enough to witness one of these snakes in the wild, be sure to keep your distance!

96. The world's oldest cat lived to reach 38 years old.

97. There is a fungus known as "dead man's fingers" that resembles decomposing human fingers emerging from the ground! When this fungus matures, it turns black and releases powdery white spores, making it appear even more eerie!

98. The average longevity of a caged animal at a zoo is 10 years longer than the average lifespan of a wild species.

99. Cats were so treasured by the Egyptians they were typically mummified after death.

100. In the world of kangaroos, male kangaroos are known as "bucks," while females are called "does" or "jills".

101. Rather than using cats to chase away pests like mice and rats, the Romans used ferrets!

102. Chameleons are the only species of lizard that are capable of seeing in both directions at the same time. The eyes of a chameleon are located on projections that look like little turrets and protrude from the animal's head. The pupil is the sole part of the eye that is visible when the cone-shaped eyelids rotate together with the eyeballs.

103. The Bronx Zoo, which is considered to be one of the largest wildlife conservation parks in the United States, is home to about 4,000 animals representing over 650 different species.

104. The name "dinosaur" originates from the Greek for "terrible lizard".

105. Apples, along with pears and plums, belong to the rose family.

106. The male peacock spider is known for its elaborate courtship dance, which involves waving its brightly colored abdomen and legs to attract a mate. These tiny spiders' impressive moves prove that size

doesn't always matter when it comes to making a big impression!

107. Mount Kilimanjaro, which is found in Tanzania, is the highest mountain on the African continent. Its elevation is approximately 5,895 meters.

108. The first modern zoo, which focused on scientific research and public education, was established in 1828 in London, England.

109. The Basenji, an African breed of dog, is often referred to as the "barkless dog" due to its unique yodel-like vocalisations.

110. The brain of a cat is 90% similar to that of a human's brain.

111. Kangaroo rats are the only species of animal that can live without water.

112. The funny-sounding bumblebee bat is a tiny creature measuring a mere 1.14 inches in length. It holds the title for the world's smallest mammal.

113. Pearls are unique among gemstones because they are formed within living organisms, specifically certain species of oysters and mollusks. When an irritant, such as a small grain of sand, enters the mollusk's shell, the creature secretes a substance called nacre to coat the irritant. Over time, layers of nacre accumulate, eventually forming a pearl.

114. Nutmeg, a popular spice used in cooking and baking, is derived from the seed of the Myristica fragrans tree, native to the Banda Islands in

Indonesia. The outer covering of the seed produces another spice called mace, making nutmeg and mace two different spices from the same plant.

115.   Greenland is the world's largest island. It is an autonomous territory within the Kingdom of Denmark, meaning it has a considerable degree of self-governance, although it still maintains close ties to Denmark.

116.   A domestic mouse excretes 40 to 100 droppings every day.

117.   The Sahara Desert, one of the driest and hottest places on Earth, was once a tropical paradise. Around 7 million years ago, the Sahara was home to lush forests, rivers, and even an ancient sea.

118.   Cheese is alive and breathing! Cheese is manufactured from milk, which contains live bacteria. Cheese is created by introducing bacteria into milk. Lactose in the milk is eaten by the bacteria, which produces lactic acid, which gives cheese its sour flavor.

119.   Yellowstone National Park is home to more than 500 active geysers. This is more than half of the world's geysers!

120.   While humans possess relatively large brains in comparison to their body size, they do not have the largest brains relative to body size among all species on Earth.

121.   The Megalodon is an extinct species of shark, and its name literally means "large teeth."

Megalodons were BIG, with some growing to potentially over 80 feet long.

122. Have you ever heard of a mangel-wurzel? It's a vegetable and a huge kind of beetroot that is closely related to the sugar beet.

123. The tradition of carving jack-o'-lanterns for Halloween is thought to have originated in Ireland.

124. Canada has more lakes than any other country in the world, with an estimated 2 million, containing about 20% of the world's fresh water.

125. Water deer lack antlers and have large tusks instead. Both males (bucks) and females have these fearsome-looking tusks!

126. Urushiol is the irritant and poison found in Poison ivy. But did you know that cashews, mangos, and pistachios are related to poison ivy?

127. Octopuses are known for their remarkable problem-solving abilities, such as unscrewing jar lids to access food.

128. In the 1800s, Dalmatians were commonly used as "coach dogs" and would run alongside carriages to guard the horses, the carriages, and the occupants from any potential dangers, including other dogs!

129. The narwhal's iconic "tusk" is actually a long, spiralled tooth that can grow up to 10 feet in length. While the exact purpose of this tooth remains a mystery, it has led to the narwhal being nicknamed the "unicorn of the sea."

130. California is responsible for the production of 98 percent of the kiwifruit that is farmed in the United States.

131. A kiwifruit has twice as much vitamin C as an orange.

132. Humans are responsible for around 85 percent of all wildfires that occur annually in the United States.

133. The English Mastiff is the biggest dog breed, weighing up to 200 pounds.

134. Cats have a specialised collar of bones in their necks called the hyoid, which allows them to meow but not roar.

135. Lion cubs are born with spots to help them blend in with the tall grass and evade predators.

136. Koalas are able to sleep for even longer than sloths and regularly sleep for 20 hours a day. This is because it takes a significant amount of energy to digest the poisonous leaves that they eat. Koalas derive almost all their sustenance from eucalyptus leaves, an impressive feat considering these leaves are laden with toxic compounds that render the plant virtually inedible to nearly all other organisms!

137. The death cap mushroom is so poisonous that ingesting just one can be fatal to humans. Despite this, some animals can eat them without harm.

138. The baobab trees of Africa can store up to 120,000 liters of water in their trunks to endure harsh drought conditions.

139.   Venus flytraps do not close randomly; they only snap shut when the tiny hairs inside their "mouths" are touched multiple times, confirming the presence of live prey.

140.   In 1943, a flock of seagulls caused a power outage in Seattle when they dropped a large number of clams onto electrical substations!

141.   The town of Talkeetna, Alaska, had a cat named Stubbs as its honorary mayor for nearly 20 years. Stubbs held the unofficial title from 1997 until his death in 2017, and during his "term," he became a beloved local figure and a popular tourist attraction.

142.   The Kakapo, a flightless parrot native to New Zealand, is known for its curious and friendly behavior, as well as its propensity to "freeze" when startled. It's also famous for its unique call, which sounds like a loud, rhythmic "booming" noise that can be heard from miles away.

143.   In 2012, a pigeon named "Pidge" in Australia became a local celebrity after it was discovered that the bird had been regularly commuting on the train. The pigeon would hop on board at a suburban station and ride to the city, hopping off at the same stop each time.

144.   The Blobfish, a deep-sea fish found off the coast of Australia and New Zealand, is famous for its unusual, gelatinous appearance. Due to its lack of muscle and skeleton, the Blobfish's body is mostly composed of a soft, jelly-like substance that helps it withstand the crushing pressure of the deep ocean.

145.   The Pygmy Marmoset, the world's smallest monkey, is native to the Amazon rainforest and weighs only 100 grams when fully grown.

146.   The Wombat, a marsupial native to Australia, is known for its cube- shaped droppings. These unique feces are believed to help mark the wombat's territory and prevent the droppings from rolling away, ensuring they stay in place as a visible signpost.

147.   The tongue of a blue whale can weigh as much as an elephant.

148.   Snails can sleep for up to three years. They enter a state of hibernation called aestivation to conserve energy during periods of extreme heat or cold.

149.   Octopuses have three hearts and blue blood. Two of their hearts pump blood through the gills, while the third circulates it throughout the body.

150.   An Octopus's blood is blue because it contains copper-rich hemocyanin, which is more efficient at transporting oxygen in cold and low-oxygen environments than hemoglobin.

151.   Lions, which are often referred to as the "kings of the jungle," are actually the second largest big cat species. Tigers are actually the largest. Adult male lions can weigh between 330 to 550 pounds (150 to

250 kilograms) and measure up to 8 feet (2.5 meters) in length, not including their tails.

152.   The scientific name for a lion is Panthera leo, which means "big cat."

153.   Bend in Oregon is home to a unique natural wonder, the world's largest petrified tree. Known as the "Petrified Log," this remarkable fossilized tree measures over 40 feet in length and is estimated to be over 5 million years old.

154.   A group or family of lions is called a pride. Prides consist of between 2 and 40 lions and these are mostly lionesses. There is usually only one dominant male lion in a pride. He is the only one that gets to mate with the lionesses!

155.   You probably already know that spider silk used to make webs and catch prey is stronger by weight than steel. Some spiders actively decorate their webs with additional silk called stabilimenta, which is used to not only catch prey, but also to attract it.

156.   Europe is home to the world's largest meteorite collection, housed in the Natural History Museum in Vienna, Austria.

157.   The world's largest model railway, known as Miniatur Wunderland, is located in Hamburg, Germany.

158.   A small village in Sweden holds an annual "Moose Dropping Festival." The event, which celebrates the region's moose population, features various moose-related activities, including a contest to guess the weight of a giant pile of moose droppings.

159.   The Phantom Kangaroo phenomenon involves reported sightings of kangaroos or wallabies outside their native habitat, particularly in North America and Europe. While some sightings have been attributed to escaped exotic pets, others remain unexplained, fuelling speculation about the origins of these mysterious marsupials.

160.   An adult giant squid's eye can grow to be as large as 30 cm (about 12 inches) in diameter, making it one of the largest eyes in the animal kingdom.

161.   Lake Tanganyika, which lies partly in Burundi in East Africa, is the longest freshwater lake in the world and the second deepest. Lake Baikal in Russia is the deepest freshwater lake at just over 1 mile deep in places!

162.   Taumatawhakatangihangakoauauotamateaturipukakapikimaungahoronukupokaiwhenuakitanatahu—a hill in New Zealand, holds the record for the longest place name in the world.

163.   People used to be buried alive by accident, which led to the implementation of safety coffins with bells.

164.   The River Thames whale, known as "Willy the Whale" by Londoners, was a young female northern bottlenose whale which made its way up the River

Thames in central London on Friday, 20th of January, 2006. I know, as I was there.

165. Acnestis is the area of the back (or backbone) between the shoulder blades that an animal cannot scratch itself.

166. Freckles occur due to an excess of melanin, the pigment responsible for the color of your hair, skin, and eyes. Produced by melanocytes in the skin, melanin serves as a protective agent against the harmful effects of ultraviolet rays.

167. The Aye-aye is a long-fingered lemur, a strepsirrhine primate native to Madagascar that combines rodent-like teeth and a special thin middle finger.

168. Despite their petite appearance, honeybees can fly at speeds of around 15 miles per hour.

169. A "smellmet" is the pungent odor that emerges after removing a helmet or cap that's been worn for a prolonged period, particularly after physical exertion that causes sweating.

170. The Mayfly has the shortest adult life span of any animal. After spending one to two years in its nymph form underwater, it emerges as an adult only to die after just a few hours or days.

171. The collective noun for a group of jellyfish is a "smack."

172. Patellar Luxation is usually referred to as a "floating knee". When some dogs run, the kneecap shifts out of place, causing pain.

173. Honey is consumed by all bee species that produce it. This is why vegans do not eat honey — when honey is taken or removed from a hive, we are effectively taking the bees' food source away from them.

174. Vicuna wool is the most expensive wool in the world and is made from the vicuna, a tiny llama-like mammal found in the Andes Mountains of Peru.

175. Indigenous peoples of North America were the first to make maple syrup. The approach was later copied by European colonists who improved the manufacturing processes.

176. Freddie Mercury had a deep affection for cats and even dedicated a song to his favorite cat, Delilah, on Queen's 1991 album "Innuendo."

177. A dog's sense of smell is up to 100,000 times more sensitive than a human's.

178. Cleopatra was known for bathing in donkey milk to maintain her youthful complexion.

179. Cats were welcomed onboard ships because of the invaluable service they offered by catching rats. Sailors believed that all cats, but particularly black cats, brought them luck at sea.

180. Gold accounts for around 0.02% of human blood.

181. Snowflakes always have six sides or "arms" due to their molecular structure. They are made of frozen water, which consists of two hydrogen atoms and one oxygen atom (H_2O).

182. Kangaroos are unable to walk backwards due to the design of their bodies.

183. A group of flamingos is called a "flamboyance."

184. A group of tigers is called a streak or ambush of tigers. Tigers can breed with other large cats, resulting in hybrids such as ligers and tigons.

185. Skin accounts for around 15% of your overall body weight, and the average person sheds an average of 1.5 pounds of skin every year.

186. The puss moth caterpillar may look soft and cuddly but has venomous spines that can cause painful stings.

187. The Giant's Causeway in Northern Ireland is a natural wonder consisting of 40,000 interlocking basalt columns, formed by an ancient volcanic eruption.

188. The River Shannon, the longest river in Ireland, was named after Sionna, a Celtic goddess. It's rumored she took a dip in the river to gain eternal wisdom, but got swept away by the current.

189. The Netherlands is the largest exporter of tulips in the world, producing more than three billion bulbs annually. Talk about a blooming good business!

190. The Chupacabra is a creature from Latin American folklore, said to be a dog-like creature that sucks the blood of livestock. Sightings of the Chupacabra date back to the 1990s, when it was first seen on the Caribbean Island of Puerto Rico. Since then, there have been numerous sightings of the Chupacabra, but no concrete evidence has ever been found.

191. Dogs are not the only "man's best friend". Humans have also been friends with cats, goats, and birds and many other animals. Goats are brilliant animals and can be trained to respond by name. I'm not sure if they can return a ball or stick, though!

192. Electric eels are capable of producing electric shocks of up to 600 volts, which is enough to stun or even kill small prey, like fish and crustaceans. In fact, this is enough to deter larger predators, like crocodiles and humans. However, they also use their electric abilities to "see" their surroundings through a process called electrolocation.

193. Some species of fish can change gender during their lifetime. This hermaphroditic trait is present in about 2% of fish species. Some species, like the Asian sheepshead wrasse, regularly transition from male to female. Clown fish start off as males before changing into females. One creature that can switch between the sexes is the goby. You may have seen gobies in rock pools by the beach.

194. Sloths are nocturnal creatures that sleep for up to 18 hours every day. Depending on the type, a sloth can have two toes with claws or three toes with claws. Sloths are related to anteaters because they both have these long, arched toenails, or claws. A baby sloth is called a calf.

195. In 1932, Australia waged a "war" against emus. Farmers in Western Australia were struggling with an influx of emus that were destroying their crops. The Australian military was called in to help, armed with machine guns! However, the emus proved difficult to catch, and the military eventually withdrew, conceding defeat to the birds!

196. Over the last decade, there has been a spike in seaweed aquaculture, fueled by a growing interest in exploiting the aquatic plant as a biofuel. Unlike land-based biofuels such as maize, soybeans, and sugarcane, seaweed does not compete with other food or non-food crops for land and fresh water.

197. Lisse Keukenhof in the Netherlands is the largest garden in the world with more than seven million flowering plants, covering an area of nearly 80 acres, or around 3 times the size of Ellis Island. So don't moan the next time you are asked to cut the grass in your garden.

198. Present-day tyres are made up of around 25% synthetic polymers (plastics) and only about 20% natural rubber, in addition to metal and other materials. Obviously, these plastics spread, not only to the immediate environment of the roads, but also by air and water thus polluting our environment with plastic waste.

199. The Bombay cat is the most common of the 22 recognized breeds of cats that have completely black coats. It is also the most popular choice of black cat. There are even specimens that have black whiskers and black paws as well.

TRANSPORTATION & TRAVEL

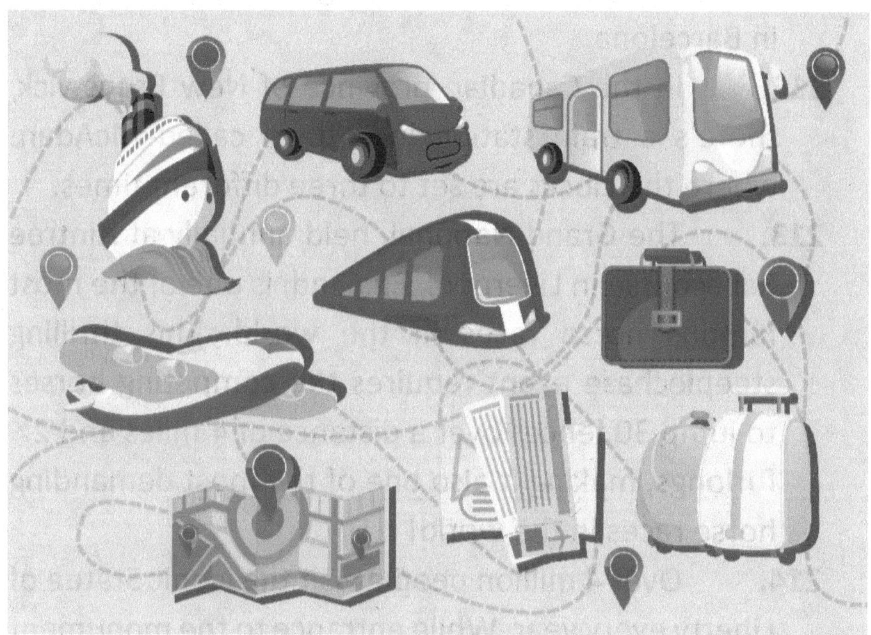

206. The Guinness Storehouse in Dublin is Ireland's most visited tourist attraction.

207. Ireland is home to the "magic road" in County Louth, where cars appear to roll uphill, defying gravity.

208. The Cliffs of Moher, one of Ireland's most iconic landscapes, have appeared in several movies, including "The Princess Bride" and "Harry Potter and the Half-Blood Prince."

209. The Danube River, Europe's second-longest river, flows through ten countries, more than any other river in the world.

210. For more than 40 years, the Ford F-150 has been the most popular truck (and car) in the U.S.

211. The Eiffel Tower was originally supposed to be in Barcelona.

212. In the Canadian province of New Brunswick, there's a train station in a town called McAdam where the clocks are set to three different times.

213. The Grand National, held annually at Aintree Racecourse in Liverpool, England, is one of the most famous horse races in the world. This thrilling steeplechase event requires the competing horses to jump 30 fences over a distance of 4 miles and 2½ furlongs, making it also one of the most demanding horse races in the world!

214. Over 4 million people visit the iconic Statue of Liberty every year. While entrance to the monument is free, visitors need to take a ferry from Manhattan to Liberty Island, which also includes a stop at historic Ellis Island.

215. Venice, Italy, is built on a series of wooden piles driven into marshy ground, a construction technique that many experts believed would cause the city to sink, eventually. However, Venice has defied the odds and continues to enchant visitors with its unique beauty and charm.

216. Japan is the undisputed vending machine capital of the world, boasting one machine for every 23 people! These convenient contraptions dispense everything from hot meals to coffee.

217. Glenwood Springs, Colorado contains the largest natural hot springs pool in the world. The pool is over 3 acres in size and contains almost 1 million gallons of water.

218. In Moncton, Canada, there's a place called Magnetic Hill, where it appears as if vehicles roll uphill when placed in neutral. While it's actually an optical illusion created by the surrounding landscape, it's still a fun and mystifying experience for visitors.

219. If you are searching for something truly unusual, you should definitely visit Valle de Luna. This bizarre and unearthly scenery is unlike anything else on Earth, and it is certainly worth a visit if you ever find yourself in Bolivia. The lunar landscape of Valle de la Luna, also known as the Moon Valley, has well and truly earned its name. You can find it at the Los Flamencos National Reserve in the Atacama Desert of northern Chile.

220. The world's largest natural mirror is the Salar de Uyuni salt flat in Bolivia. Spanning over 4,000 square miles, this salt flat becomes a giant mirror during the rainy season when a thin layer of water transforms it into a surreal landscape.

221. There's a giant pineapple-shaped building in Bathurst, South Africa. Standing at 55 feet tall, the "Big Pineapple" is a tribute to the region's pineapple industry and even features an observation deck at the top. Who wouldn't want a birds-eye view from a giant pineapple?

222. Dollywood, the theme park owned by Dolly Parton, is situated in Pigeon Forge, Tennessee. The Park attracts more than three million people each year.

223. The most expensive automobile ever sold at auction is the Ferrari 250 GTO, which fetched $70 million.

224. The island of Barbados is really two coral reefs! The northern section is termed the Scotland District, while the southern part is known as the St. James District.

225. Giethoorn, a picturesque village in the Netherlands, is often referred to as the "Venice of the North" because it has no roads

226. The world's steepest street, according to the Guinness World Records, is Baldwin Street in Dunedin, New Zealand, with a gradient of 35% at its steepest section.

227. The first vehicles used as taxis in the City of London were known as hackneys. The word "hacquenee" originated in France and meant that a horse could be rented. The name is still very much in use today, particularly those of an older generation, and people continue to refer to a taxi as a "hackney cab."

228. There were ever only 20 commercial Concorde aircraft produced. Concorde could take off at 250 mph and cruise at more than twice the speed of sound. On the 24th of October 2003, the last commercial Concorde flight flew from New York to Heathrow.

229. The world's largest airport terminal is located at the Beijing Daxing International Airport in China, which was designed by Zaha Hadid. The terminal covers an area equivalent to 144 football fields

230. The first pallet patent was issued in 1925 to Howard Hallowell, who called it a "Lift Truck Platform". They are now used for stacking, storing, and transporting almost all of the products we buy.

231. In the early 20th century, the "Flying Tank" was designed as a hybrid between a tank and an aircraft, intended to provide the military with a heavily armed vehicle that could fly to the battlefield. The concept proved to be too heavy and impractical, and the Flying Tank never made it off the ground.

232. The world's oldest public railway line that is still in operation today is the Middleton Railway in Leeds, England. It was first established in 1758 as a wooden waggonway using horse-drawn carts, and it later transformed into a steam-powered railway in 1812.

233. The famed Orient Express, a luxury train service that once connected Paris to Istanbul, first began operations in 1883.

234. The city of Venice, Italy, is famous for its intricate network of canals, but it is also built on more than 100 small islands connected by over 400 bridges.

235. The Trans-Siberian Railway spans almost the entire length of Russia, covering a distance of over 9,000 kilometers, making it the longest railway line in the world.

236. Singapore's Changi Airport is frequently voted the world's best airport, featuring a butterfly garden, a rooftop swimming pool, and a four-story slide.

ARCHITECTURE

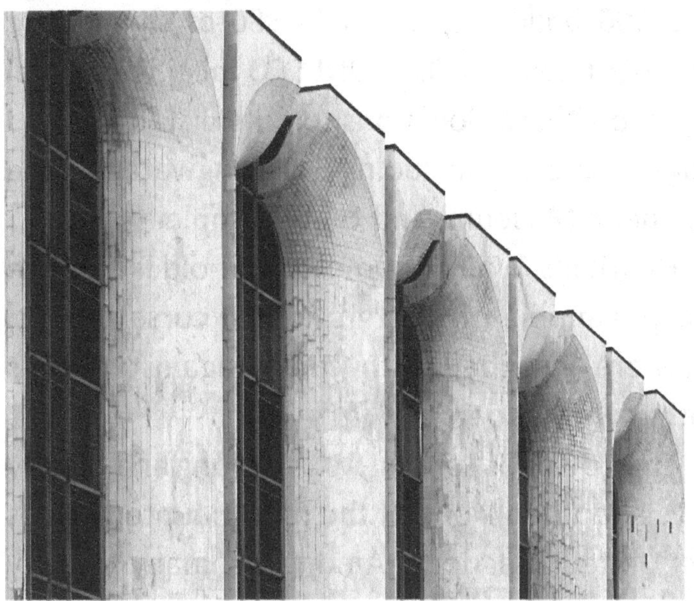

237. The historic Tower of London was built in the 11th century and is now one of the most popular tourist attractions in London. Every day in London, for more than 700 years, the gates at the Tower are locked during the "Ceremony of the Keys."

238. Constructed in 1967 as a unique centennial project, the world's first UFO landing pad is located in St. Paul, Alberta. This pioneering initiative was designed to showcase Canada's open-mindedness and receptiveness to the possibility of extraterrestrial life.

239. At 73 miles long, Hadrian's Wall in the United Kingdom is the longest surviving Roman defensive structure in the world.

240. The prolific architect Frank Lloyd Wright was known for his groundbreaking designs. He designed around 800 buildings, but only 380 of them were ever constructed. In 2019, UNESCO included a total of eight of these locations on its list of World Heritage sites, including Fallingwater, the Guggenheim Museum, and Unity Temple.

241. Hadrian's Wall is home to the oldest known surviving example of written Roman curse tablets, which were inscribed with curses against thieves and other wrongdoers.

242. The Tower of London, with its long and bloody history, is reputedly one of the most haunted places in the United Kingdom. Among its many ghostly residents are the headless Anne Boleyn, the Princes in the Tower, and the White Lady, who is said to have been spotted many times in the White Tower.

243. The iconic White House has been the official home and workplace of every U.S. President since John Adams in 1800. This historic building, situated at 1600 Pennsylvania Avenue in Washington D.C., has witnessed more than two centuries of presidential history!

244. The Statue of Liberty's index finger is 8 feet long.

245. The Park Theatre, which opened in 1732, was the earliest Broadway theatre.

246. The Great Wall of China, one of the world's most iconic landmarks, isn't actually a single, continuous wall. Instead, it's a collection of walls and fortifications constructed over centuries by various dynasties.

247.   626. Mount Rushmore National Monument in South Dakota contains the sculpted faces of four past Presidents of the United States. They are George Washington, First President of the United States. Thomas Jefferson, Third President of the United States. Theodore Roosevelt, 26th President of the United States, and Abraham Lincoln, 16th President of the United States.

248.   Brasília, nestled in the heart of Brazil, is actually the country's capital and not Rio de Janeiro! Brasília was inaugurated in 1960 and replaced Rio de Janeiro as the nation's capital of the time.

249.   Famous Egyptian designer and builder Imhotep, served Pharaoh Djoser, and is the reputed architect of the Djoser step pyramid. Imhotep's actual historical significance at the time is mostly unknown, but throughout the 3,000 years that followed his death, he underwent an elevation to God-like status within historical Egyptian culture.

250.   The 456-foot-tall doors that are on NASA's Vehicle Assembly Building at Kennedy Space Center in Florida, are officially the tallest doors in the world.

251.   Any rug larger than 40 square feet is classified as a carpet.

252. The Burj Khalifa in Dubai, at over 828 meters tall, is the world's tallest building, with 163 floors above ground.

253. Antoni Gaudí's Sagrada Família in Barcelona has been under construction since 1882 and is still incomplete, with completion aimed for 2026 to coincide with the centenary of Gaudí's death.

254. In 1941, a bombing raid destroyed the chamber of the House of Commons in London. It was rebuilt based on plans made by architect Giles Scott who also designed the Battersea power station. Giles is also credited with designing the much-loved red telephone boxes that are seen all over the capital.

255. Tower Bridge, an iconic symbol of London, is not only a marvel of engineering but also a master of disguise! Many people often mistake it for London Bridge, its less extravagant neighbor.

256. The Leaning Tower of Pisa was never intended to tilt. The tilt began during construction, caused by an inadequate foundation on ground too soft to properly support the structure's weight.

257. Completed in 1894, Tower Bridge in London features a unique design that includes a pair of bascules, which are the massive, movable sections of the roadway. These bascules can be raised in just five minutes to allow river traffic to pass beneath, creating a striking visual spectacle for onlookers.

258.   Londoner, Charles Barry, won a competition in 1835 to redesign Westminster Palace after a fire in the previous year. Charles Barry was already a well-known architect, having built many churches, buildings, and gardens that we see in the capital today.

259.   The Citadel of Aleppo, situated in Syria, is considered the world's oldest castle, boasting construction elements that date back to 3000 BC. This ancient fortress reflects the various civilizations that have inhabited the region throughout history.

260.   The Winchester Mystery House in San Jose, California, is an architectural marvel with labyrinth-like interiors, staircases that lead to nowhere, and doors that open to blank walls. The sprawling mansion was built by Sarah Winchester, heiress to the Winchester rifle fortune, who believed that continuous construction would appease restless spirits.

261.   The Coral Castle in Florida, USA, is an enigmatic stone structure built single-handedly by Edward Leedskalnin between 1923 and 1951. How Leedskalnin managed to move and carve the massive blocks, weighing several tons each, remains a mystery.

262.   Windsor Castle, constructed in 1070 AD, stands as the oldest castle still in use today. As a royal residence for over 900 years, it has certainly witnessed significant events and transformations throughout British history!

263.   The Danyang-Kunshan Grand Bridge in China presently (2023) holds the world record for the world's longest bridge, measuring a mind-blowing 104 miles long.

264.   The Trans-Siberian Express was built between 1891 and 1916 under the instruction of Russian Tsars Alexander III and his son Nicholas II.

265.   It took fourteen years to build the Sydney Opera House. Work began in 1959 and required over 10,000 construction workers to finish what is widely regarded as one of the finest buildings of the twentieth century.

266.   American singer Paul Robeson was the inaugural performer at the Sydney Opera House. He serenaded the construction workers with "Ol' Man River" during their lunch break.

267.   France gifted the Statue of Liberty, officially titled "Liberty Enlightening the World," to America as a symbol of the centennial celebration of Franco-American friendship. Frederic Bartholdi designed the statue, while the renowned French engineer Gustave Eiffel, who also designed the Eiffel Tower, created its structure.

268.   The Gateway Arch, often referred to as the Gateway to the West, is a notable landmark situated on the western bank of the Mississippi River in St. Louis, Missouri. Standing at an impressive 630 feet tall, it holds the distinction of being the tallest arch in the world.

269. The faceless clock at Salisbury Cathedral in Wiltshire in the UK, is the world's oldest remaining functioning clock, believed to date from 1386 or possibly even earlier.

270. The world's longest tunnel is in Laerdal, in Norway. At almost 16 miles long, it connects the Norwegian towns of Laerdal and Aurland. It takes, on average, a good 20 minutes to drive through the tunnel.

271. Istana Nurul Iman Palace, the official palace of Brunei's Sultan, is the world's largest "house", spanning over 2 million square feet. To put that into context that's about 2.5 times bigger than Buckingham Palace.

272. Prague Castle is the world's largest castle.

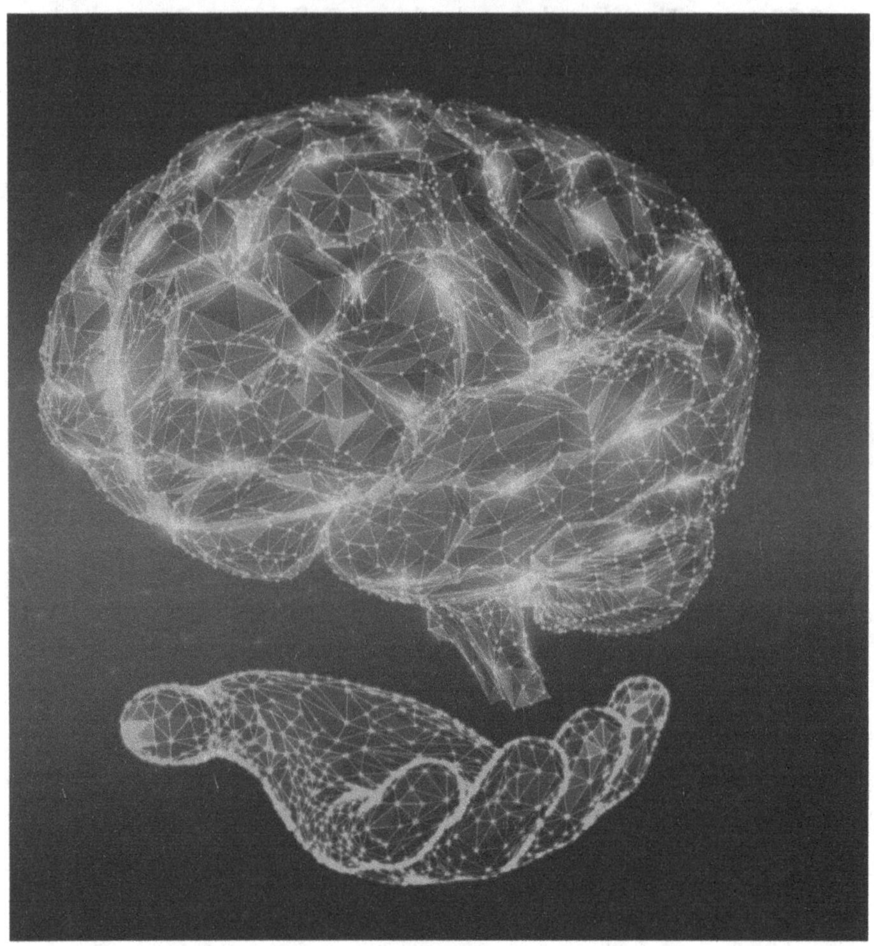

273. The human brain is around 2% of the body's total weight but uses around 20% of the body's total energy.

274. Despite being called "floppy" disks, these storage devices were actually quite rigid, with the name coming from the flexible disk inside.

275. Neil Armstrong left his boots on the moon to offset the weight of moon rocks he brought back.

276. The first-ever email spam was sent in 1978 promoting a new computer system.

277. Living on the moon would be tough. Temperatures near the lunar equator reach a sweltering 120 degrees Celsius during the day, but drop to a frosty -130 Celsius at night.

278. In 1956, the first VCR, called the Ampex VRX-1000, was invented. It was so large and heavy that it required a small team to move it around!

279. For a rocket to break free from Earth's gravity, it must reach a mind-boggling speed of 7 miles per second. This incredible velocity, known as the escape velocity, allows spacecraft to overcome our planet's gravitational pull and venture into outer space.

280. When SMS (Short Message Service) was first introduced, it was intended as a backup communication method when phone calls weren't possible. However, texting quickly became popular and now billions of text messages are sent every day, making it one of the most used communication methods worldwide.

281. In simply terms, a petabyte is 1,000 times larger than a terabyte, which is itself 1,000 times larger than a gigabyte. A petabyte is enough to store 50 billion pages of standard typed text.

282. The first recorded use of the word "selfie" was in an Australian internet forum in 2002.

283. When threatened, the bombardier beetle can release a scalding, foul-smelling spray from its abdomen to deter predators. This chemical reaction is so powerful that it can produce an audible sound when released.

284. Between 24 to 140 vibrations per second have been observed in a house cat's purr.

285. The term "pixel" is derived from "picture element," and it was first coined in 1965.

286. Did you know that Google Chrome has a hidden dinosaur game?

287. The "@" symbol, now commonly used in email addresses, has a mysterious history.

288. The term "pixel" is derived from "picture element," and it was first coined in 1965.

289. The total amount of code written for Google's services and applications is over 2 billion lines of code.

290. Fact 920: Humans have already begun preparing for Mars' colonization with simulations conducted on Earth.

291.   Fact 924: Quantum levitation is a fascinating phenomenon where superconducting materials can float over a magnetic source due to the Meissner effect and quantum locking.

292.   Hidden 100 metres underground near Geneva, Switzerland, the Large Hadron Collider (LHC) holds the title of the world's most powerful particle accelerator. This remarkable machine can propel particles at nearly the speed of light.

293.   Helium is the element with the least amount of mass.

294.   The Sun makes up over 99% of the total mass of our solar system.

295.   Sound travels about four times faster in water than in air, making the ocean a sonic superhighway!

296.   During a search for extraterrestrial life, a signal from deep space that lasted for 72 seconds was heard. No one has ever explained the signal, nor was it ever received again. No wonder they called it the "wow" signal!

297.   To ensure that the crew of the British-designed Centurion tank never ran out of hot tea, a boiler was installed inside. It ran off the vehicle's electrical systems

298. The cerebrum is the largest part of the brain and is responsible for conscious thought, perception, and voluntary movement.

299. In 2017, scientists successfully teleported a photon from Earth to a satellite in orbit over 500 kilometers away, using quantum entanglement.

300. Sunflowers are known to "follow" the sun through a process called heliotropism.

301. On Mars, sunset is blue due to the way the planet's atmosphere scatters light from the sun.

302. Our understanding of DNA has revealed that humans share approximately 50% of our DNA with bananas.

303. The Large Hadron Collider (LHC) at CERN is the world's largest and most powerful particle accelerator.

304. The first electric light was demonstrated in Newcastle upon Tyne, United Kingdom, by Sir Joseph Swan in 1879.

305. It is estimated that there are more stars in the universe than there are grains of sand on all the world's beaches.

306. Timekeeping is a complex science, but one of the most precise clocks in existence is the atomic clock. Using the vibrations of cesium atoms, these clocks can be accurate to within a fraction of a second over millions of years.

307. In the 1960s, LED technology was so new that a single LED would cost around $200. Now, LEDs are commonplace and found in many everyday devices like smartphones, TVs, and light bulbs.

308. The internet was originally called ARPANET (Advanced Research Projects Agency Network) and was first connected in 1969 as an experiment by the U.S. Department of Defense.

309. The term 'robot' was first used to denote a fictional humanoid in a 1920 Czech language play. The word 'robot' comes from the Slavic word 'robota,' which means forced labor or drudgery.

310. Morse code, which was widely used for long-distance communication in the early part of the 20th century, uses dots and dashes to represent letters and numbers. It was created in the 1830s by Samuel Morse and Alfred Vail.

311. Wi-Fi isn't short for "Wireless Fidelity." It's simply a trademarked term meaning IEEE 802.11x.

312. The very first domain name ever registered was Symbolics.com, on March 15, 1985.

313. ENIAC, short for Electronic Numerical Integrator and Computer, was the first programmable, general-purpose electronic digital computer, built in 1945-46.

314. Blockchain is a system of recording information in a way that makes it difficult or impossible to change, hack, or cheat the system. A blockchain is essentially a digital ledger of transactions that is duplicated and distributed across the entire network of computer systems on the blockchain

315. Because of its antibacterial qualities, sulfur dioxide is occasionally used as a preservative for dried fruit such as apricots and is known in Europe as E220.

316. Tungsten has the highest boiling point of all the elements and can tolerate temperatures of up to 5,000 degrees Celsius. Even lava is not hot enough to boil Tungsten.

317. Light travels at a constant speed of around 186,000 miles per second

318. In the early days of computing, the term "debugging" was taken quite literally when engineers found an actual moth causing problems in the hardware. This event, involving a moth found in a relay of a Mark II computer in 1947, was documented by computer scientist Grace Hopper and her team.

319. The brain has the ability to generate new cells and connections, a process called neuroplasticity, which helps people adapt to changes and learn new things.

320. The brain's memory capacity is practically limitless.

321. Arteries and veins play distinct roles in the circulatory system: arteries transport oxygen-rich blood away from the heart to supply the body's tissues, while veins return oxygen-depleted blood back to the heart for re-oxygenation.

322. A robot was chosen to carry the Olympic torch in South Korea in 2018.

323. The first SMS message was sent over the Vodafone GSM network in the United Kingdom on 3 December 1992. The message read "Merry Christmas."

324. The human body contains enough DNA that if unwound and linked together, it would stretch across the solar system multiple times.

325. Water bears, or tardigrades, are microscopic creatures known to survive extreme conditions, including the vacuum of space.

326. The melody and tune of the Star-Spangled Banner are taken from the English drinking song "To Anacreon in Heaven."

327.   Blood is about six to eight percent of body weight.

328.   The 8th of May is considered World Red Cross and Red Crescent Day.

329.   Antibiotics, though prevalent now, were a significant discovery that has saved countless lives since their introduction.

330.   Aspirin, derived from the bark of willow trees, was one of the first painkillers and is still used today.

331.   The first recorded car theft occurred in Paris in 1896. The Peugeot, owned by Baron de Zuylen, was stolen by his mechanic.

332.   The first SMS was sent in 1992 and said, "Merry Christmas."

333.   The first webcam was used in 1991 at Cambridge to monitor a coffee pot.

334.   The Voyager 1 spacecraft carries a gold-plated audio-visual disc in the event that it is found by intelligent life forms from other planetary systems.

335.   The SR-71 Blackbird holds the record for a manned air-breathing engine aircraft speed of Mach 3.3.

336.   The concept of "Herd Immunity" was first recognized as a natural phenomenon in the 1930s.

337.   The Ozone layer hole reached its largest size in 2000, covering 11.4 million square miles.

338.   The modern USB was introduced in 1996, simplifying the connection between computers and peripheral devices.

339.   The first mobile phone call was made by Martin Cooper in 1973.

340.   The Concorde was so fast that it could outrun the sun, and passengers could witness two sunsets in one day.

341.   The first computer virus was created in 1971, named the Creeper system.

342.   The Deepwater Horizon oil spill is the largest marine oil spill in history, with the equivalent of approximately 4.9 million barrels of oil discharged.

343.   Due to refraction in the atmosphere the sun seems slightly flattened when near to the horizon.

344.   In 1979, the Skylab space station's re-entry into Earth's atmosphere caused widespread panic and speculation about where debris would land. The San Francisco Examiner even offered a $10,000 reward to the first person who could deliver a piece of Skylab to their office within 72 hours of the crash. A 17-year-old Australian named Stan Thornton won the prize after finding a chunk of the space station in his backyard.

345. The International Space Station is the most expensive object ever constructed, at a cost of $150 billion.

346. Nikola Tesla proposed the concept of wireless charging over a century ago.

347. The largest recorded digital data breach involved the compromise of 3 billion Yahoo accounts.

348. The lightning strike that hit the Apollo 12 shortly after its launch could have been catastrophic but ended up having minimal impact on the mission.

349. Google started as a research project by Larry Page and Sergey Brin while they were Ph.D. students at Stanford University.

350. Halley's Comet is only visible from Earth every 75-76 years.

351. Apollo astronauts trained for microgravity by walking sideways on a tilted plane.

352. The title of the longest-running laboratory experiment goes to the Pitch Drop experiment, which has been running since 1927.

353. Pencils can write in zero gravity, underwater, and on almost any surface.

354. The first message sent via the internet was "lo" as in "login," but the system crashed before the full message was completed.

355. Drones are increasingly being used for tasks such as delivery, surveillance, and photography.

356. Dendrochronology is the study of tree rings.

357. "Moon trees" were grown from seeds that the Apollo 14 mission took to the moon in early 1971. NASA, together with the U.S. Forest Service wanted to find out if the moon's orbit changed how the seeds grew on earth.

358. Psilocybe azurescens, also known as "Flying Saucer Mushrooms" are the most powerful hallucinogenic mushroom known. Ingestion can result in vomiting, drowsiness, weak muscles, and a total lack of coordination. Not recommended.

359. Belladonna drops were used by Roman ladies to make their pupils appear bigger. Belladonna is a toxin, so this practice did not continue for too long.

360. Earthworms have the astonishing capacity to repair the majority of their bodies if harmed. Earthworms have a separate head and tail, and while the head may regenerate a new tail, the tail cannot regenerate a head. Planarian flatworms are even more amazing and have the potential to regenerate into two or more new worms after being severed.

Planarian flatworms can regenerate an entire body from a cut section as little as 1/300th of the original worm.

361.   The quietest room on Earth, known as an anechoic chamber, is located at Laboratories in Minneapolis, Minnesota. With a background noise level of -9 decibels, it's so quiet that you can actually hear your own heartbeat and stomach gurgling.

362.   Did you know that the earliest known use of a prosthetic device dates back to over 3000 years ago? A prosthetic toe made of wood and leather was found on an Egyptian mummy and is thought to be one of the earliest functional prosthetic devices.

363.   Gamma-ray bursts (GRBs) are the most powerful explosions in the universe, emanating from massive stars collapsing into black holes. Scientists are still trying to fully understand these fascinating cosmic events.

364.   Telephones have been a vital part of global communication since the 1870s when Alexander Graham Bell was awarded the first US patent for the invention of an "improvement in telegraphy" which allowed for voice transmission over wires.

365.   William Grove, a Welshman from Swansea, conceived the first fuel cell concept in 1838. Subsequently, in 1932, Francis Bacon developed the first hydrogen-oxygen fuel cell. Despite these early innovations, fuel cells took over a century to find commercial applications. From the mid-1960s onward, NASA has employed the alkaline fuel cell, also known as the Bacon fuel cell, to power satellites and space capsules.

366. The first true Harley-Davidson motorbike, designed by William Harley and Arthur Davidson, was finished in 1904. At the time, they entered a motorcycle race with their prototype vehicle. Unfortunately, they came fourth.

367. In 2011, a Swedish man-made headlines when he was arrested for attempting to construct a nuclear reactor in the confines of his own kitchen! Not surprisingly, this unusual and potentially dangerous endeavor captured the attention of both the authorities and the public.

368. Lightbulb inventor Thomas Edison also designed an "electric pen" that wrote by repeatedly punching microscopic holes in paper similar to a tattoo gun. While it never really took off, Edison sold the patent, which would later be used in the first conventional office copy machine.

369. Before the Qwerty keyboard, the layout on typewriters was alphabetically organized. This annoyingly allowed for rapid typing of the popular letter combinations, resulting in key jams. The qwerty keyboard was specifically created to minimize this key clash. Genius.

370. The Titanic had a total lifeboat capacity for 1,178 people, which was more than the legal requirement at the time of her maiden voyage in 1912. However, the ship could carry over 3,300 passengers and crew, meaning the lifeboats available were not sufficient for everyone on board.

371. The SR-71 Blackbird holds the record for the fastest air-breathing manned aircraft, achieving speeds over Mach 3. It was used by the United States Air Force for reconnaissance missions and was retired in 1999.

372. AI (artificial intelligence) has made significant strides in recent years. AI systems have not only mastered games like chess and Go but have also shown to be capable of more complex tasks like protein folding prediction.

373. One of the most important scientific achievements of the 20th century was the discovery of penicillin by Alexander Fleming in 1928. This groundbreaking antibiotic has saved countless lives since its introduction.

374. Human-induced pluripotent stem cells (iPSCs) were first generated by Shinya Yamanaka's lab in 2006. These cells are derived from skin or blood cells that have been reprogrammed back into an embryonic-like pluripotent state, allowing them to become any type of cell in the body.

375. In 2003, the human genome was completely sequenced, providing a roadmap of human DNA. This monumental scientific achievement has opened up countless avenues of research into genetic diseases and personalized medicine.

376. The theory of plate tectonics is a scientific breakthrough that revolutionized our understanding of Earth's geology. It explains the movement of the Earth's lithosphere, which has important consequences for geologic events and phenomena such as earthquakes and volcanic activity.

377. Water on Mars is a subject of much scientific inquiry and speculation. There is evidence to suggest that Mars once had a much warmer and wetter climate, which could have supported life.

378. In the animal kingdom, the chameleon is renowned for its ability to change color. This remarkable adaptation is used for communication and temperature regulation, not just camouflage as commonly believed.

379. The first successful vaccine was developed by Edward Jenner in 1796 against smallpox. This innovation not only helped eradicate smallpox but also laid the foundation for modern vaccinology.

380. A black hole is a region of space where the gravitational pull is so strong that not even light can escape it. The boundary beyond which light cannot escape is known as the event horizon.

381. The concept of zero as a number was revolutionary in mathematics. Originating from the Indian mathematician-astronomers, it was later transmitted to the Islamic world, and then to Europe.

382. Quantum computing is an area of computing focused on developing computer technology based on the principles of quantum theory. Quantum computers would theoretically be able to perform certain calculations much faster than traditional computers.

383. The Doppler Effect is the change in frequency of a wave in relation to an observer who is moving relative to the wave source. It was first proposed by Austrian physicist Christian Doppler in 1842.

384. The Periodic Table of Elements, created by Dmitri Mendeleev in 1869, organizes chemical elements according to their atomic number, electron configurations, and recurring chemical properties. It is a foundational tool in chemistry and science education.

385.   Antibiotic resistance is a growing problem worldwide. It occurs when bacteria evolve and become resistant to the drugs used to treat the infections they cause, leading to more difficult-to-treat diseases and increasing the risk of disease spread, severe illness, and death.

386.   The first photograph taken by a human of Earth's view from space was captured by a camera on the V-2 No. 13 rocket on October 24, 1946. This marked the beginning of an era of space photography and exploration.

387.   Elon Musk's company SpaceX has made significant advancements in reusable rocket technology. This innovation aims to reduce the cost of space travel and make it more accessible. SpaceX has already achieved several milestones, including the first privately funded spacecraft to reach orbit and safely return to Earth.

388.   The Great Oxygenation Event, which occurred around 2.4 billion years ago, was a time when the Earth's atmosphere and the shallow ocean experienced a rise in oxygen levels. This event is among the most significant in Earth's history as it led to more complex life forms that rely on oxygen for metabolism.

389.   The Hubble Space Telescope was launched into low Earth orbit in 1990 and remains in operation. It has provided some of the most detailed visible-light images from space, leading to many breakthroughs in astrophysics and cosmology.

390.   The transistor, a semiconductor device used to amplify or switch electronic signals and electrical power, is one of the key active components in practically all modern electronics. It was invented by William Shockley, John Bardeen, and Walter Brattain at Bell Labs in 1947.

391.   In 1956, the academic discipline of artificial intelligence research was established. The four main categories of AI now recognized are reactive AI, limited memory AI, theory of mind AI, and self-aware AI. In Saudi Arabia, the realistic humanoid AI called Sophia was awarded citizenship in 2007! Sophia does exhibit certain traits that could be classified as "theory of mind" AI.

392.   Douglas Engelbart created the first computer mouse in 1964. It was made of wood.

393.   Joe Breeze, who unveiled the Breezer Series 1 in 1978, is largely credited with creating the first specifically designed mountain bike. The Breezer, often regarded as the first modern mountain bike, was constructed using chromoly, which is much stronger than conventional steel.

394.   Although there are several variations on this fundamental semiconductor, gallium arsenide is the substance that is most frequently utilized in LEDs and many other electronic devices.

395.   Quantum computing represents a new paradigm in computational capability, leveraging the principles of quantum mechanics to process information at speeds exponentially faster than current computers.

BUSINESS, ECONOMY & WORK

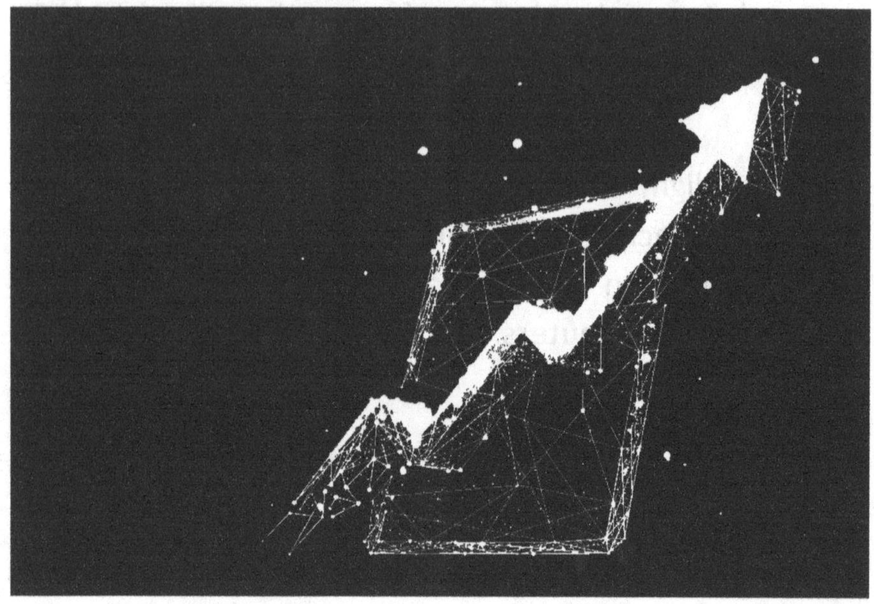

396. In 2012, thieves stole approximately 3,000 tons of maple syrup worth $18 million from a warehouse in Quebec, Canada. The heist was eventually discovered, and many of the perpetrators of this bizarre crime were arrested.

397. China is credited with the first mass manufacture of steel. It created complex state-operated iron foundries as early as the 5th century BC.

398. A victualler is someone who supplies food, drinks, and other supplies to the crew of a ship while it is at sea.

399. The Four interlocking rings on Audi cars symbolise the merging of four vehicle manufacturers—Audi, DKW, Horch, and Wanderer.

400. The first commercially successful video game was Pong, an arcade table tennis game released by Atari in 1972.

401. An unhealthy dependence on cheese is possible. Casein, one of the proteins found in cheese, has the potential to be addictive!

402. According to estimations provided by the International Dairy Federation, France is currently in first place for having the highest annual per capita consumption of cheese, while Italy comes in a close second.

403. In 1814, a large vat at the Meux and Company Brewery in London ruptured, releasing over 1.2 million litres of beer. The flood destroyed several buildings and sadly killed eight people. The incident became known as the Great London Beer Flood, a tragic but peculiar event in the city's history.

404. It was the Ottoman Turks who initially brought coffee to Constantinople. Kiva Han, the first coffee shop in the world, opened its doors in Turkey in 1475.

405. Leo Fender, an American inventor and entrepreneur, revolutionized the music industry with his electric guitars and amplifiers. He founded Fender Electric Instrument Company in 1946 and introduced the iconic Telecaster and Stratocaster guitars.

406. North Carolina, Kentucky, and Virginia are the three most important states in terms of tobacco production in the United States.

407. The highest-grossing video game franchise of all time is Pokémon, with over $100 billion in revenue across games, merchandise, movies, and other media.

408. The Swiss franc is considered one of the most stable currencies in the world, thanks to Switzerland's strong economy and low inflation.

409. The krona is the currency of Sweden, "krona" means "crown" in Swedish.

410. Vatican City has its own unique economy with a population of around 800 people and even its own postal system!

411. Sliced bread was first manufactured by a machine and sold commercially in the 1920s by the Chillicothe Baking Company in Missouri.

412. The Diamond Hope necklace takes its name from Henry Philip Hope, the owner of the diamond at that time. The story behind the diamond before this is shrouded in some mystery. It was originally stolen in 1791 from India by the French gem trader. Shortly after this, he became afflicted with a severe fever, and died. Other tales tell of him being attacked and killed by a pack of hungry wolves. However, there are other accounts that claim he lived quite happily until the age of 84! Many people believe that the Hope Diamond is cursed and anyone linked with the diamond will either suffer a dreadful death or be struck by ill luck.

413.   The majority of Wasabi consumed is not genuine Wasabi, but rather a concoction of horseradish, mustard, and green food colouring. The reason being is that authentic wasabi is prohibitively expensive!

414.   Did you know that Azerbaijan had the world's first oil well? The country has a lengthy history with oil, extending back to the nineteenth century.

415.   Cryptocurrency "mining" is so called because it is similar to mining precious metals in that it requires exertion and slowly yields new currency at a rate that mimics the rate at which commodities like gold are mined from the ground.

416.   The Canadian dollar, also known as the "loonie," features an image of a loon on one side, which is a type of waterbird found in Canada.

417.   Swansea in Wales was once the copper capital of the world in the 18th and 19th centuries. At its peak, 90% of Britain's copper-smelting capacity came from the Swansea area, which was known at the time as "Copperopolis."

418.   Silicon Valley in California is named after the silicon used in semiconductor devices and is considered the global center for high technology and innovation.

419.   The concept of the "gig economy" gained traction in the 21st century, emphasizing flexible, freelance, or temporary jobs often connected with technology platforms.

420.   Sir Hiram Maxim was a British-American inventor who is best known for making the first automatic portable firearm—otherwise known as the machine gun. Maxim had patents for many other devices, including the gun silencer, the mousetrap, and a device for curling hair.

421.   Percy Shaw was an English businessman and inventor who, in 1934, was granted the patent for the cat's eye reflective road stud. The idea came to him after driving down a steep twisting road one misty night in 1933.

422.   Major George Howson founded the "Poppy Factory" in London in 1922 to employ injured veterans to provide employment for veterans injured during the First World War. A unique feature of the poppy is that it can be assembled with only one hand, allowing injured veterans to make them.

423.   In 2022, U.S. stock markets accounted for roughly 60% of global stock markets. Japan was the second largest stock market country, followed closely by the United Kingdom.

424.   The Industrial and Commercial Bank of China Ltd is currently the world's largest bank in terms of total assets under management. The bank offers services to large corporations and "high-net-worth" individuals.

425. A New Yorker, known as the "Artichoke King", once bought all the artichokes that were transported to New York from California. He later resold the artichokes for massive profits. Eventually, the mayor of New York had to step in and announced a total ban on artichokes in an attempt to curb this unethical profiteering. However, one week later, the mayor decided to back down after admitting he was quite partial to artichokes himself.

426. The global financial crisis of 2007-2008 is considered by many economists to be the worst financial crisis since the Great Depression of the 1930s.

427. During the 18th and 19th centuries, London's Covent Garden was synonymous with the sex industry. The area was full of brothels, and the infamous Harris's List of Covent Garden Ladies, a directory of London prostitutes, was published annually from 1757 until 1795.

GEOGRAPHY

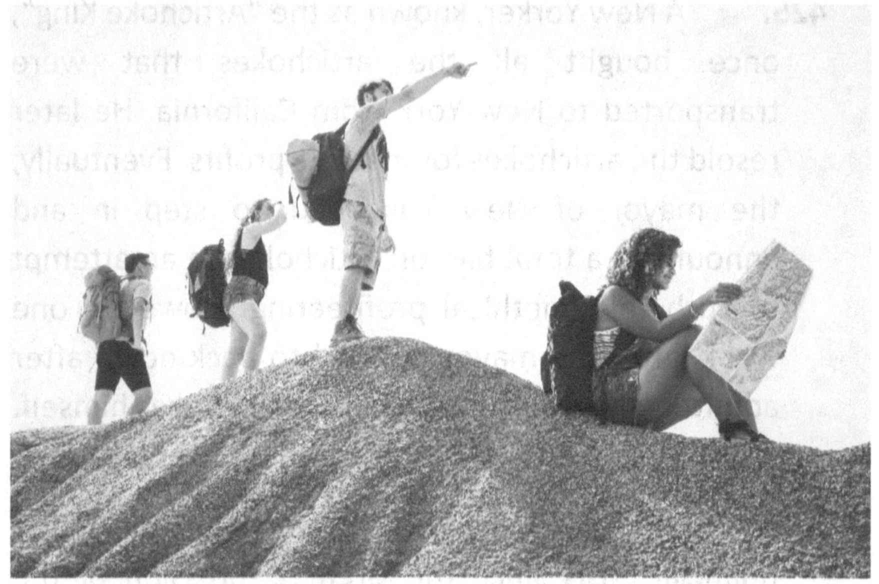

428. The Danube River, Europe's second-longest river, flows through ten countries, more than any other river in the world.

429. The famous Appalachian Trail is a 2,175-mile long hiking trail that connects Mount Katahdin in Maine to Springer Mountain in Georgia. It stretches over 14 states. It was completed in 1937 and is now maintained entirely by volunteers.

430. Africa has Arabic, English, French, Portuguese, Swahili, and Zulu as its official languages.

431. Mount Fuji, Japan's highest peak, isn't just an impressive natural landmark—it's also a magnet for tourists from around the world!

432.   The "Manneken Pis"—the statue of a boy weeing, is one of Brussels' most recognised sights!

433.   With a population of more than 8.5 million in 2023, New York is the most populous city in the U.S. Los Angeles and Chicago are the next most populous.

434.   According to the findings of a recent study, there was a Viking settlement in North America one thousand years ago, which is several centuries before Christopher Columbus arrived in the Americas. A new method of dating that relies on the analysis of tree rings has reportedly supplied proof to the scientific community that Vikings inhabited a site in Newfoundland, Canada, in the year 1021 AD.

435.   The world's biggest gold nugget was unearthed in Australia and weighed a staggering 62 kg.

436.   Afghanistan is home to the world's highest capital city, Kabul, which sits at an elevation of approximately 5,900 feet above sea level. The city is surrounded by the Hindu Kush Mountain range.

437.   The continents are constantly on the move, albeit very slowly. At the current rate of about 1 to 2 inches per year, it would take about 300 million years for New York and London to become neighbors.

438.   France is also home to the highest mountain peak in Europe. Mont Blanc, situated in the French Alps, rises at a staggering 4,810 metres tall.

439. The United States is the fourth largest country in the world, after Russia (1st), Canada (2nd), and China (3rd).

440. The title for the world's foggiest place goes to the Grand Banks, a region in the Atlantic Ocean situated near the shores of Newfoundland.

441. Africa is the only continent that spans both the northern and southern temperate zones and is located in all four hemispheres: north, south, east, and west.

442. Alaska manages to be both the westernmost and easternmost state in the United States!

443. Russia spans across 11 time zones, making it the country with the most time zones in the world.

444. The town of Baarle is a peculiar case of intertwined borders between Belgium and the Netherlands.

445. Monaco is the world's second-smallest country by land area, measuring just 2 square kilometers.

446. Delaware may be the second smallest state in the US, but it holds the impressive title of "The First State". This historic moment happened on December 7th, 1787.

447. From "The First State" (Delaware in 1787), to the final state (Hawaii in 1959), each state has a distinct history, terrain, and cultural legacy—each is a separate entity as well as part of the country.

448. The United States is home to a larger immigrant population than any other nation.

449. Garrison Dam was responsible for creating Lake Sakakawea—the biggest artificial lake in the United States.

450. The Pacific Ocean holds the distinction of being the Earth's largest and deepest ocean, encompassing over half of the planet's total ocean water volume. The Pacific Ocean is larger than all of the Earth's landmass combined!

451. Greenland is the world's largest island. It is an autonomous territory within the Kingdom of Denmark, meaning it has a considerable degree of self-governance, although it still maintains close ties to Denmark.

452. The state of Oklahoma has the highest concentration of natural lakes of any other state in the United States.

453. The Pacific Ocean's "Ring of Fire" is a massive horseshoe-shaped area that is home to 75% of the world's volcanoes and experiences 90% of the Earth's earthquakes. The Ring of Fire is formed by the boundaries of several tectonic plates that meet and interact in the Pacific Ocean, creating a zone of intense geological activity.

454. The Sahara Desert makes up approximately 80% of Algeria.

455. Mount Everest is located in Nepal and is the tallest mountain in the world. The peak was given its name in honour of George Everest, who served as Surveyor General of India in the nineteenth century.

456.   The River Ganges, or Ganga, is the third-largest river in the world. It stretches just over 1,500 miles from its source in the western Himalayas in India to its delta in the Bay of Bengal in Bangladesh.

457.   The River Thames, sometimes referred to as the River Isis, is the second longest river in England. It stretches an impressive 215 miles, and is surpassed only by the River Severn.

458.   Due to its lush green scenery, Ireland is commonly referred to as the "Emerald Isle".

459.   Louisiana is known as the Pelican State because of its official state bird.

460.   The Congo River, which travels across Africa, is the world's deepest river.

461.   Bolivia has the highest navigable lake in the world—Lake Titicaca

462.   Asia Minor, or Anatolia, is a huge peninsula in Western Asia and the most westerly extension of the Asian continent. Today, it makes up the bulk of the country of Turkey.

463.   The shortest war in history was between Britain and Zanzibar on August 27, 1896. Zanzibar surrendered after 38 minutes.

464.   The Pacific Ocean contains around 25,000 islands.

465.   Java holds the distinction of being the world's most populous island, accommodating over half of Indonesia's population.

466.   In Europe, there are more than 200 officially recognised languages!

467.   The microstate of Andorra, nestled in the Pyrenees mountains between Spain and France, has one of the highest life expectancies in the world. It seems that mountain air and a relaxed lifestyle are the secrets to longevity!

468.   The oldest known tree in Europe, nicknamed "Adonis," is a Bosnian pine located in Greece. It's estimated to be over 1,075 years old, standing tall as a living witness to centuries of history.

469.   The small, landlocked country of Luxembourg is the only remaining Grand Duchy in the world, a title held by the ruling Grand Duke or Duchess.

470.   The tiny European country of San Marino, completely surrounded by Italy, claims to be the world's oldest republic, having been founded in 301 CE.

471.   The Channel Tunnel, also known as the "Chunnel," is an underwater rail tunnel connecting England and France. Completed in 1994, it is just over 31 miles long.

472.   The Dead Sea is one of the world's saltiest bodies of water, which allows people to float effortlessly due to the high buoyancy.

473. Lake Baikal in Russia is the world's deepest and oldest freshwater lake, containing around 20% of the world's unfrozen freshwater reserve.

BOOKS & LITERATURE

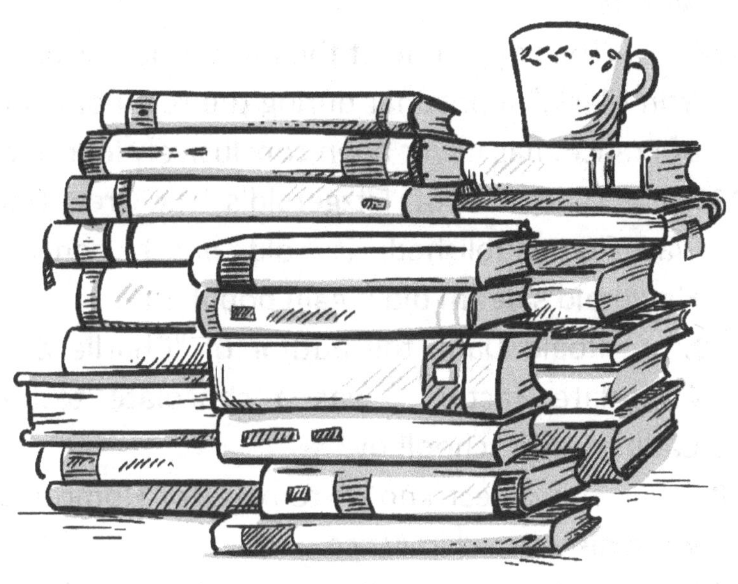

474. The Irish language, known as Gaeilge, is one of the oldest written languages in the world.

475. Bram Stoker's 'Dracula' was inspired by several quoted sources, including the historical figure Vlad the Impaler, Irish folklore, and even a nightmare induced by eating too much crab meat.

476. The longest palindrome in the English language is "tattarrattat," a word coined by James Joyce in his novel Ulysses.

477. It is estimated that The Bible was authored over a span of 1500 years by more than 40 distinct writers.

478. The true name of the mysterious "Man in the Iron Mask," a prisoner during the reign of Louis XIV of France, has never been conclusively identified.

479. When F. Scott Fitzgerald's "The Great Gatsby" was first published, it sold poorly; only after Fitzgerald's death did it gain popularity.

480. Roald Dahl, the author of "Charlie and the Chocolate Factory," was a chocolate tester for Cadbury as a schoolboy.

481. The oldest known remains of Homo sapiens were discovered in Africa.

482. In the early 20th century, the small town of Tenino, Washington, faced economic collapse when its only bank failed. To save the local economy, the town began issuing its own currency made from wood. The wooden money became a novelty, attracting tourists and helping the town recover from the crisis.

483. King George VI of the United Kingdom was known for his stutter, which made public speaking a challenge for him. His efforts to overcome his speech impediment were famously depicted in the film "The King's Speech."

484.   The name "Bible" derives from the Greek word biblia, which means "books".

485.   The town of Springfield, where "The Simpsons" is set, was intentionally given a generic name so that viewers could imagine it being located anywhere in the United States. Matt Groening has said that he named it after Springfield, Oregon, a town close to his hometown of Portland.

486.   When it was first published in 1897, "Dracula" received mixed reviews and only moderate commercial success. It wasn't until the 20th century, with the rise of vampire-themed movies and television shows, that the novel gained widespread recognition and became a classic.

HISTORY, CULTURE & SOCIETY

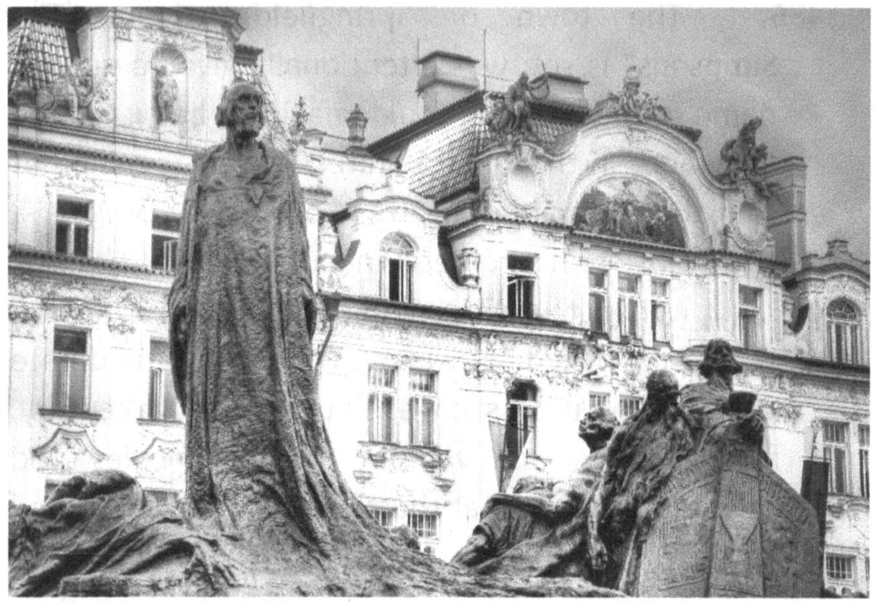

487. Whilst on a sea voyage to Rhodes, the then 25-year-old Julius Caesar was attacked, captured, and then held to ransom by Cilician pirates.

488. While Venice is famous for its canals, Birmingham in the United Kingdom actually has more miles of canals than the Italian city.

489. Mauna Loa is dwarfed by the extinct Puhahonu volcano, which is the largest single-volcano in the world.

490. The Christmas tree tradition originated in Germany.

491. Children in Germany receive their Christmas stocking on Saint Nicholas Day, which is on December 6th.

492. The national animal of Canada is the beaver and can be found on the Canadian nickel (5-cent coin) and the Canadian coat of arms.

493. In 622 AD, the Quba Mosque in Medina was constructed. It is the first mosque for which an exact date can be established. It is also described in the Islamic holy book, the Quran.

494. In 1866, the tiny European country of Liechtenstein sent 80 soldiers to fight in the Austro-Prussian War. They returned home with 81 soldiers, having suffered no casualties and having made a new Italian friend along the way.

495. Althing is the name of the oldest parliament in the world, which is located in Iceland. It was constructed in 930 AD.

496. Albert Einstein declined the Israeli presidency.

497. Benito Mussolini wrote The Cardinal's Mistress—a romantic book.

498. The rich history of the United States dates back to 1776, when the country was founded.

499. A baker's oven was supposedly the origin of the great fire that ravaged London in 1666.

500. Genghis Khan created a tax law that meant that certain people and professions did not pay tax. This included the poor, teachers, artists, and professions involving the law.

501. Hadrian's Wall was known by several names throughout history, including the Latin "Vallum

Aelium" (Aelian Wall), named after Emperor Hadrian's family name, Aelius.

502. Historians are of the opinion that Genghis Khan was responsible for the establishment of one of the world's first international postal systems.

503. Some of the most accomplished architects and engineers of their time were the ancient Mayans.

504. The Battle of Bosworth Field, fought in August of 1485, marked the end of the Wars of the Roses and the rise of the Tudor dynasty.

505. Australia's origins as a penal colony date back to 1788 when the British established the first settlement to alleviate overcrowding in English prisons.

506. Ellis Island, which opened its doors on January 1, 1892, played a pivotal role in shaping the United States as we know it today.

507. During the French Revolution, a new calendar was adopted and utilized for the next 12 years, from 1793 to 1805.

508. While studying at a prestigious British institution, Winston Churchill picked up the habit of smoking. As time went on, he decided to switch from cigarettes to cigars. Following his time in Cuba, he became a lifetime fan of Romeo y Julieta and La Aroma de Cuba cigars.

509. The Roman Empire, one of history's most formidable forces, held sway over an expansive realm that stretched from Britain to North Africa and from Spain to the Middle East at its peak!

510.   Age-wise, sharks have been around longer than trees.

511.   According to the results of a DNA analysis, the mysterious King Tut's parents were first cousins.

512.   John Lennon suffered from poor eyesight throughout his life. Without his eyeglasses, he would have been judged to have legal blindness according to today's criteria

513.   The city of Vienna, Austria, consistently ranks as one of the world's most livable cities, thanks to its high quality of life, rich culture, and efficient urban planning.

514.   The country of Bhutan measures its progress and success by Gross National Happiness rather than Gross Domestic Product, emphasizing the well-being of its citizens over economic growth.

515.   A "blue moon" is the term for the second full moon in a single calendar month. It is a relatively rare event, leading to the phrase "once in a blue moon" to describe infrequent occurrences.

516.   Cleopatra reigned from 51 BC to 30 BC, almost 2,500 years after the construction of the Great Pyramid of Giza.

517.   During the 17th and 18th centuries in Europe, fox tossing was a popular sport among the nobility. It consisted of a single person or a pair throwing a fox as far and as high as they could.

518.   The Comanches, sometimes known as the "Lords of the Plains," were considered to be among the most fearsome Native American tribes during the time of the American frontier.

519.   Armenia was the first country to adopt Christianity as the state religion in 301 AD.

520.   The Europeans brought smallpox to the Americas, and it was this disease that was responsible for the greatest number of fatalities and sickness among the indigenous people.

521.   Known for his toughness and determination, Roosevelt was once shot in the chest by a would-be assassin while delivering a campaign speech in Milwaukee, Wisconsin, in 1912.

522.   Pi is an infinite, non-repeating decimal, meaning that every possible number combination exists somewhere in pi, including potentially your phone number and date of birth.

523.   The concept of "left" and "right" politics originated during the French Revolution, relating to the seating arrangement in the Estates General.

524.   The "Hollywood Walk of Fame" features over 2,500 terrazzo and brass stars embedded in the sidewalks along 15 blocks of Hollywood Boulevard and three blocks of Vine Street in Hollywood, California.

525.   April 21 is celebrated as "Kindergarten Day" to recognize Friedrich Froebel, who began the first kindergarten in 1837 in Germany.

526.   The first item sold on eBay was a broken laser pointer for $14.83.

527.   "Chuseok," also known as Korean Thanksgiving Day, is one of the most important and festive holidays of the year in Korea

528.   Basketball, the beloved sport around the world, was invented by a Canadian PE teacher James Naismith, in 1891.

529.   In 1963, Major League Baseball pitcher Gaylord Perry joked that a man would walk on the moon before he hit a home run.

530.   Baseball's first recorded game took place in 1846 in Hoboken, New Jersey.

531.   The first Olympic Games in modern history were held in Athens, Greece, in 1896.

532.   In Ashanti culture (present-day Ghana), the Golden Stool is believed to contain the soul of the Ashanti people.

533.   The shortest-serving U.S. President was William Henry Harrison, who died of pneumonia just 32 days into his term

534.   Amelia Earhart made history in 1928 by being the first woman to fly alone across the Atlantic Ocean.

535.   The English monarch Elizabeth I did not marry, nor did she have any children.

536.   By the time the war ended in 1945, the United States Army had 12,000,000 enlisted men and women under its command.

537. The bacterium Yersinia pestis was responsible for the Black Death. This was a bubonic plague epidemic that killed millions in Europe and Asia in the 14th century.

538. Greeneville, South Carolina, takes its name from the prominent American revolutionary commander Nathanael Greene.

539. The War of 1812 lasted for two and a half years, from June 1812 to February 1815. Despite its name, the war did not end in 1812 but continued on into the subsequent years, with significant battles occurring in 1813 and 1814.

540. It is estimated that around 98% of history has been lost throughout time.

541. The first people to occupy the Americas were the American Indians. The precise date is unknown, although they are thought to have crossed the Bering Strait from Asia more than 10,000 years ago.

542. Tennessee's official nickname is The Volunteer State, in honor of the thousands of Tennesseans who volunteered to fight in the War of 1812.

543. Queen Victoria held the record for the longest reigning monarch in English history with 63 years and 7 months on the throne. However, Queen Elizabeth II broke the record in 2015.

544. The earliest evidence of alcohol manufacturing can be found in China, when rice wine was manufactured approximately 7000 BC.

545.   Skirts were considered masculine in Ancient Greece. In fact, Greeks considered pants or trousers to be effeminate and they would insult any man who wore them!

546.   Scientists examining the sand on Normandy's beaches discovered minuscule fragments of smoothed-down shrapnel from the D-Day landings.

547.   Caligula, the Roman Emperor, appointed one of his favourite horses to the position of senator.

548.   Feng Shui is an ancient Chinese philosophy that focuses on designing and arranging buildings, rooms, and furniture in harmony with the natural world to promote positive energy, or "chi."

549.   The Maori people of New Zealand traditionally greet one another with a "hongi," which involves the pressing together of one's nose and forehead to another person. This gesture is akin to a handshake in Western culture but is believed to convey the sharing of one's breath of life.

550.   The average person in the United Kingdom drinks around 876 cups of tea per year—that's more than any other nation in Europe!

551.   It's thought that throwing coins into a fountain for good luck originated with the ancient Celts. It was believed that since water was a gift from the gods, giving them a gift in return by tossing coins could appease them and ensure good fortune.

552.   April Fools' Day dates back to the 1500s when the Western world switched from the Julian calendar, which observed the new year at the end of March, to the Gregorian calendar, which designated January 1st as the new year. Those who continued to celebrate the new year in spring were called April Fools.

553. Tattooing has been practiced across the globe since at least Neolithic times, as evidenced by mummified preserved skin and ancient art. The oldest discovery of tattooed human skin to date is found on the body of Ötzi the Iceman, dating from between 3370 and 3100 BC

554. The unicorn is the national animal of Scotland. It may seem unusual for a country to choose a mythical creature as its national symbol, but the unicorn was chosen because it represents purity, innocence, power, and strength. Scottish kings believed that having a unicorn in their coat of arms would ensure their reign's prosperity and success.

555. Elvis Presley enlisted in the United States Army in 1958, in Memphis, Tennessee. His active duty ended in 1960.

556. Leonardo da Vinci never attended school.

557. Louisiana was named after King Louis XIV in 1682, when France acquired the territory.

558. Haiku is a form of Japanese poetry that traditionally consists of three lines with a 5-7-5 syllable pattern and typically reflects on nature or the seasons.

559. The Yucatan Peninsula was named after a misunderstanding. Spaniards asked the locals what their region was called. The locals replied "Yucatan," which in their language meant "I don't understand you."

560. The outbreak of World War II prevented a UK census from being conducted that year.

561. Chopin, the Polish composer and pianist, requested that his heart be removed and returned to his native Poland after his death.

562. The first country to implement universal suffrage (the right to vote for all adults) was New Zealand when it granted women the right to vote in 1893.

563. The French erected a "fake Paris" towards the end of WWI, complete with a Champs-Elysées and the Gare du Nord look-alike.

564. The Greeks were responsible for inventing the lifting apparatus known as the crane, which they named after the bird due to its resemblance.

565. As far as the public knows, the United States has never reached DEFCON 1. The closest the nation is believed to have come to this level was during the Cuban Missile Crisis, when it reportedly reached DEFCON 2.

566. The tradition of brides wearing white on their wedding day was popularized by Queen Victoria in the 19th century. Before that, brides simply wore their best dress, regardless of color.

567.   In Denmark, it is a tradition for those who are unmarried at 25 to get cinnamon thrown all over them on their birthday.

568.   Earth isn't a perfect sphere but rather an oblate spheroid.

569.   In the remote Norwegian town of Longyearbyen, it is illegal to die.

570.   The word "robot" comes from the Czech word "robota," which means "forced labor" or "servitude." The term was first used in the 1920 play "R.U.R." ("Rossum's Universal Robots") by Karel Čapek.

571.   The Great Wall of China is not a single continuous structure but a collection of walls and fortifications built over various dynasties, primarily as a defense against northern invasions

572.   A tradition in Spain involves eating twelve grapes at midnight on New Year's Eve, one for each chime of the clock, to bring good luck for the upcoming year.

573.   The oldest known joke dates back to 1900 BC and suggests that toilet humor was as appreciated in ancient times as it is today.

574.   Although Genghis Khan is revered as a national hero in modern Mongolia, his name was forbidden during Soviet rule.

575.   The Great Wall of China is not a single, unbroken wall but a series of walls and fortifications, with some parts dating back to the 7th century BC.

576. The Rosetta Stone, now housed in the British Museum, was the key to deciphering Egyptian hieroglyphs, providing texts in three scripts which allowed translation.

577. In the year 776 BC, the first Olympic Games were held. Competitors in the original ancient Olympic Games were expected to take part naked.

578. Betsy Ross is widely credited with designing and creating the first American flag, known as the "Stars and Stripes," which she presented to George Washington in 1776.

579. During the Cold War era, the United States developed a plan called "Project A119," which aimed to detonate a nuclear bomb on the Moon as a show of strength against the Soviet Union. The project was never carried out.

580. The Indian Citizenship Act, passed by Congress in 1924, was the first step toward granting citizenship to Native Americans.

581. The Principality of Sealand claims to be the smallest country in the world with its own flag, currency, and "royal family."

582. Constantinople was renamed Istanbul in 1930.

583. The English word "algebra" comes from the Arabic word "al-jabr," which means "the reunion of broken parts," reflecting the discipline's objective to solve for unknowns.

584. After the Battle of Gettysburg, local farmers discovered that their wheat and corn crops were more robust than ever before. This was due to the fact that the plants were nourished by the remains of soldiers buried just below the surface.

585. Alchemy contributed to the development of early chemistry in the Islamic world during the 8th to 14th centuries.

586. The phrase "the luck of the Irish" may have originated from the discovery of gold and silver by Irish miners in the 19th century.

587. The first mention of tablecloths in history was ascribed to a poet named Martial in the beginning of the first century.

588. Thomas Alva Edison is best known for inventing domestic light bulbs and the electric power system.

589. A stevedore is a waterfront worker who traditionally helps load and unload ships or boats.

590. The "Kilroy was here" graffiti became popular during WWII, symbolizing the presence and influence of American culture.

591. In ancient Rome, urine was used as a teeth whitener and mouthwash due to the ammonia content acting as a cleaning agent

592. In Japan, KFC is a popular Christmas Eve dinner, thanks to a successful marketing campaign in the 1970s.

593. The ancient city of Athens, Greece, is home to the world's first known democracy, established around 500 BC.

594. The world's oldest surviving amusement park, Bakken, is located just outside of Copenhagen, Denmark. It opened in 1583!

595. The world's first postage stamp, the Penny Black, was issued in the United Kingdom in 1840. It revolutionised the postal system and made sending mail more affordable and accessible to people around the globe.

596. The tradition of throwing coins into a fountain stems from the ancient practice of gifting water deities with offerings, usually in the form of precious metals, for safe travel over water.

597. The Maasai people in Kenya greet each other by spitting. For them, it's a sign of respect and good fortune.

598. In New Zealand, a traditional Maori greeting involves pressing one's nose and forehead to another person's in a "hongi."

599. Amish communities choose not to use modern technology not because they don't understand it, but because they believe it creates inequality.

600. The name "Bluetooth" technology is derived from the 10th-century Scandinavian King Harald Bluetooth who united Denmark and Norway, as Bluetooth technology was designed to unify different devices.

601. Oktoberfest in Munich, Germany, originally started as a horse race to celebrate the Bavarian crown prince's wedding in 1810.

602. The "keep calm and carry on" poster was originally created by the British government in 1939 to boost morale in the event of a wartime disaster.

603. The Lotus position, often associated with meditation, has been used for thousands of years and is rooted in the meditative practices of ancient India.

604. Tipping is a practice that originated in Tudor England. "To insure promptitude," TIPS, was a phrase used in coffeehouses, where coins would be dropped into a box to ensure that wealthy customers received better service.

605. "The Great Bath" is part of the ancient city of Mohenjo-Daro in Pakistan and is considered to be the earliest public water tank in the ancient world.

606. The use of "blue blood" to denote nobility comes from the Spanish phrase "sangre azul." It reflects the fact that the old nobility of Castile refrained from marrying those considered to have darker skin, such as the Moors and Jews, maintaining the paleness (and thus the visibility of blue veins) in their skin.

607. The fedora hat has its name derived from the title of an 1882 play by Victorien Sardou, "Fédora", in which the main character, Princess Fédora Romanoff, wore a hat similar to it.

608. The peace symbol we use today was designed in 1958 by Gerald Holtom for the British nuclear disarmament movement. It is a combination of the semaphore signals for the letters "N" and "D," standing for "nuclear disarmament."

609. "Bloody Sunday" refers to two events: one in Ireland in 1920 and another in Northern Ireland in 1972. Both events were characterized by excessive violence leading to deaths, and are considered pivotal in the history of Irish nationalism.

610. The Berlin Wall was a symbol of the Cold War and divided Berlin both physically and ideologically for 28 years. It was the most palpable manifestation of the Iron Curtain and served as the most prominent symbol of the division between East and West Germany until its fall.

611. In 1794, during the height of the French Revolution, the French government decided to abandon the traditional seven-day week in favor of a ten-day week. This system, part of a larger effort to de-Christianize the calendar, lasted until Napoleon Bonaparte abandoned it in 1805.

612. In 1787, King Frederick William II of Prussia created a fake army to trick neighboring countries into believing Prussia had a larger military force.

613. Before refrigeration, Russians kept milk fresh longer by placing a brown frog in it.

614. The Terracotta Army was discovered in 1974 by local farmers in Lintong District, Xi'an, Shaanxi province, China.

615. The American Civil War had more casualties than any other U.S. war, and its Battle of Gettysburg was the deadliest.

616. Wolfgang Amadeus Mozart transcribed Gregorio Allegri's "Miserere" at the age of 14 after hearing it only twice.

617. Napoleon may not have been as short as commonly believed, partly due to measurement differences between the English and French yardsticks.

618. The story of Pandora's box comes from Greek mythology and teaches about human curiosity and temptation.

619. Joseph Haydn's head was stolen from his grave for phrenology studies and was returned over 150 years later.

620. The Romans developed metal locks and keys, and the "warding system" for security.

621. Orson Welles' radio adaptation of "The War of the Worlds" in 1938 caused widespread panic among listeners.

622. The Dutch National Lottery is the oldest continuing lottery, having been established in 1726.

623. Pelé won his first World Cup at the age of 17 and was also born with an extra toe due to polydactyly.

624. The island of Bermeja was rediscovered submerged under the ocean after being thought to have disappeared.

625. A Japanese soldier remained hidden for 29 years after WWII, not realizing the war was over until 1974.

626. Sir Alexander Fleming discovered penicillin after finding mold killing bacteria in his uncovered petri dish.

627. The term "sneaker" was created to describe quiet rubber-soled shoes.

628. The Great Wall of China is not visible from space with the naked eye.

629. During the American Civil War, the Union soldiers wore blue, and the Confederate soldiers wore gray.

630. Ancient Egyptians worshipped cats and punished those who harmed them.

631. Greek fire was a medieval incendiary weapon whose composition remains a mystery today.

632. The earliest recorded instance of a diamond engagement ring was in 1477, given by Archduke Maximilian of Austria to Mary of Burgundy.

633. Guglielmo Marconi sent the first wireless signal across the Atlantic in 1901.

634. After the 1917 Russian Revolution, Russia's official calendar was changed from the Julian to the Gregorian

635. The Irish invented the submarine. John Holland from County Clare designed the first functional underwater vessel in 1878.

636. Shrapnel is named after its inventor, Henry Shrapnel. Henry was an officer in the British Army who invented the concept of the "shrapnel" shell.

637. In 1823, British explorer Alexander Laing was attempting to reach the fabled city of Timbuktu when he took a wrong turn and ended up in the Sahara Desert! Despite the setback, Laing eventually reached his destination, becoming the first European to do so.

638. It is often quoted that the Great Fire of London, which lasted for 5 days in 1666, killed 6 people. However, many historians argue that this is likely to be unfortunately untrue because the fire destroyed all traces of life, and many more people would have perished without being accounted for.

639. The Japanese imperial dynasty is said to have begun in 660 BC, making it the oldest monarchy in the world.

640. Grigori Rasputin was a legendary figure in Russian history, and his life was filled with many interesting stories. He had a reputation for being a mystic who had magical powers and could cure people of illnesses. He was also known for his wild behavior, often involving drinking and partying with the Russian elite. He became friends with the last

Russian Tsar, Nicholas II, and his wife Tsarina. There are many myths and legends about Rasputin, but the one thing that is true is that he remains a fascinating and enigmatic figure in popular culture!

641. Damascus is the capital of Syria and is one of the world's oldest cities to have been inhabited continuously. The city is mentioned in the Bible's book of Genesis.

642. Renaissance artist Michelangelo was born in 1475, in the town of Caprese Michelangelo, in Italy's Tuscany region. The town is named after him, not the other way around!

643. The Netherlands and the Isles of Scilly, located off the coast of Cornwall in the United Kingdom, are said to have engaged in a bloodless war for 335 years. This war, of sorts, started during the English Civil War and lasted until a peace treaty was signed 335 years later! It would therefore be recognized as having lasted the longest in human history. However, doubts have been raised surrounding the legitimacy of this war. It has therefore been questioned whether a state of war actually even existed!

644. Leo Tolstoy, the Russian author best known for his novels "War and Peace" and "Anna Karenina", is regarded as the master of realistic fiction and without doubt one of the finest writers in history. Leo Tolstoy had real-life personal experience with both the military and combat, having been in the army for approximately five years and served during the Crimean War.

645. The capital of Wyoming is Cheyenne. It is also the largest city in the state. Work on the Wyoming State Capitol building in Cheyenne began in 1869, but it took a further 21 years for Wyoming to become recognized as a state.

646. One of the most brutal and well-known battles in history was the Battle of Waterloo in 1815. Did you know though, German troops accounted for around half of Wellington's British army? Significant numbers of Dutch and Belgian soldiers also took part on the victorious British side.

647. Genghis Khan, the leader of the Mongols, grew up in obscurity but went on to build the largest contiguous empire in history. His real name was Temujin. Genghis Khan was not given the honorary name he is known for until 1206 when he was appointed the leader of the Mongols.

648. It is actually the British Empire that holds the record for the world's largest noncontiguous empire in history. The British Empire spanned more than 22% of the earth's surface at one point. In 1938, the empire contained over 450 million people, which at the time was around 20% of the global population.

649.   The real Captain Morgan (the same name as a famous rum) was a Welsh privateer who fought alongside the English in the Caribbean against the Spanish. Sir Henry Morgan was his official full name and title. He was knighted by King Charles II.

650.   The longest year on record occurred in 46 BC. To adjust the calendar for his calendar reform, which became effective in 45 BC, Julius Caesar added three extra intercalary months for that year. As a result, the year of 46 BC had 445 days! This year was known as the "annus confusionis," which is Latin for "year of confusion." It is recognized as the longest calendar year in human history.

651.   The "War of the Bucket" or "Battle of the Bucket" was fought in 1325 between the rival city-states of Bologna and Modena. It was triggered by Modena's forces stealing a large wooden bucket from Bologna. Despite the seemingly trivial cause, the war was a significant conflict during the intercity rivalry era in Italy.

652.   In Switzerland, it's illegal to own just one guinea pig because they're social animals and considered victims of abuse if they are alone.

RELIGION

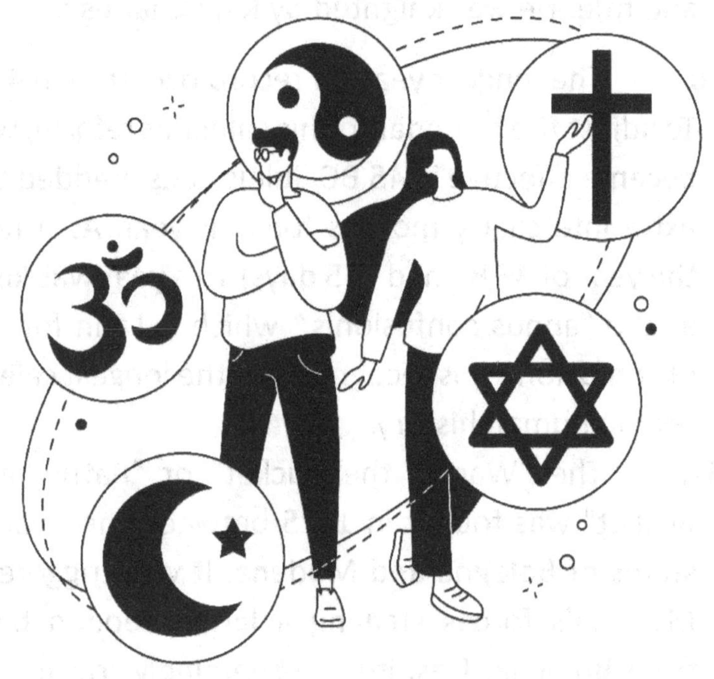

653. Brunei's official religion is Islam, and the country has some of the toughest religious compliance rules in the world. For example, the sale of alcohol and tobacco in Brunei is prohibited.

654. In folklore, crossroads are often depicted as magical or haunted places. One of the most famous tales is that of Robert Johnson, a blues musician who is said to have sold his soul to the Devil at a crossroads in exchange for musical talent.

655.   Cleopatra was not from Egypt, she originated from Macedonian Greece. Her family ruled Egypt for over three centuries, and she was the first of her line to learn the Egyptian language.

656.   The "Marcha Real" is the national anthem of Spain and is notable for being one of the few patriotic anthems that does not contain any lyrics at all.

657.   The famous philosopher, Socrates, never wrote any books and all that is known about him and his teachings come from his students like Plato

658.   Because of its singular approach to economic growth based on the concept of Gross National Happiness, Bhutan is often thought of as one of the happiest countries on the globe.

659.   The Bible has been translated into over 2,000 distinct languages.

660.   The Four Noble Truths are an essential teaching in Buddhism, summarizing the essence of Buddhist thought.

661.   The Kaaba, located in Mecca, is considered the most sacred site in Islam. Muslims around the world face the Kaaba during their five daily prayers.

662.   The Vatican City, the smallest independent state in the world, has a population of about 800 and an area of 44 hectares.

663.   The construction of Stonehenge in England began around 3000 BC and continued in phases until about 1600 BC. The purpose of this ancient monument has been a subject of speculation and study for centuries. Some theories suggest it was used as a burial ground, while others propose it was a place for healing or astronomical observation.

664.   The Church of the Nativity in Bethlehem is one of the oldest continually operating churches in the world and stands over the cave that tradition marks as the birthplace of Jesus.

665.   The word "set" has the highest number of different meanings in the English language.

MUSIC, ARTS, SPORTS, FASHION & ENTERTAINMENT

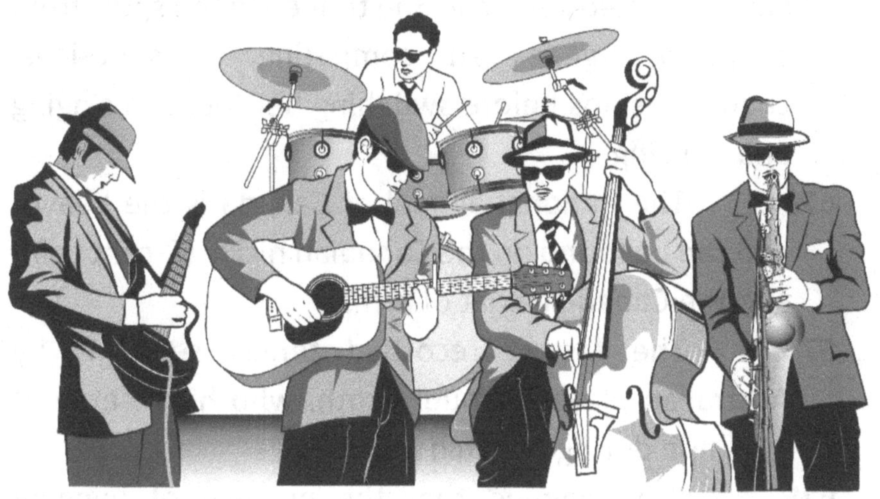

667. The Super Bowl is the most-watched sporting event in the United States.

668. The harp is the national symbol of Ireland, and it's the only country in the world to have a musical instrument as its national symbol.

669. Ireland is known for its unique sports, like Gaelic football and hurling, which are both fast-paced and highly skilled games.

670. Vienna, Austria, is known as the "City of Music" due to its rich musical heritage. Composers such as Mozart, Beethoven, and Strauss have deep connections with the city.

671.   Matt Groening's father inspired the naming of the character Homer in "The Simpsons". They share the same name!

672.   Before becoming a pop star, Britney Spears was a talented gymnast. She trained in the sport from a young age, even competing in state-level championships before switching her focus to singing and dancing.

673.   The national animal of Canada is the beaver and can be found on the Canadian nickel (5-cent coin) and the Canadian coat of arms.

674.   The fastest recorded tennis serve is by Australian player Samuel Groth, who hit a serve at 163 mph during a match in 2012.

675.   It is claimed that the practice of hanging stockings beside the fireplace on Christmas Eve stems from a tale about Saint Nicholas, who is said to have placed gold coins in the stockings of three needy sisters.

676.   In certain cultures, wishing someone good luck is considered unlucky. Because it is believed that by doing so, one tempts fate.

677.   James Cameron drew the charcoal portrait of Kate Winslet that was included in the film Titanic.

678.   In the original novels by Ian Fleming, James Bond's signature drink was not the martini that he's famous for ordering in the movies, but rather a mix of gin and tonic.

679.   The first recorded use of the word "soccer" was in 1863 in England, where it was coined as a shortened form of "association football" to distinguish it from other forms of football.

680.   The 1980s saw a revolutionary collaboration with the Reserve Bank of Australia resulting in the creation of plastic bank notes! These durable, innovative notes made their debut in 1988 with the introduction of the $10 bill.

681.   Former President Jimmy Carter had a hidden talent as a Grammy-winning storyteller. Carter has won no less than three Grammy Awards in the Best-Spoken Word Album category for his works!

682.   Steven Spielberg was the executive producer for the original "Back to the Future" movie, which was a massive success, grossing over $381 million worldwide.

683.   During his lifetime, Vincent van Gogh only had one sale, and that was of "The Red Vineyard at Arles," and it was to a friend.

684.   Whitney Houston's version of "I Will Always Love You" is a cover. The original version was sung by Dolly Parton.

685.   President Lincoln was an enthusiastic wrestler before he became the 16th President of the United States. Out of 300 bouts, he only had one loss.

686.   With over 100 million albums sold worldwide, the Armenian-American singer Cher is one of the most successful singers of all time.

687. Tetris, the popular tile-matching video game, became so addictive that players would see falling blocks in their peripheral vision and dream about the game. This phenomenon became known as the "Tetris effect".

688. Bridesmaids and groomsmen in early Anglo-Saxon weddings were called "bride's knights" and "groom's knights." They had the responsibility of protecting the happy couple from danger during the wedding festivities!

689. Did you know that Google Chrome has a hidden dinosaur game? When you're offline and see the "Unable to connect to the Internet" screen, press the spacebar to start a simple, fun game featuring a running dinosaur. It's a quirky way to pass the time when the internet is down.

690. The slow loris, a small nocturnal primate, is one of the few venomous mammals. Its toxin is produced by glands on its elbows, which it licks or rubs on its head for self-defense.

691. Eddie "The Eagle" Edwards, the British ski jumper, captured the world's imagination at the 1988 Winter Olympics in Calgary. Despite finishing last in both of his events, Eddie's fearless spirit and underdog story won him a special place in the hearts of fans everywhere.

692. Tarantulas may look scary with their large size and hairy legs, but most species are not dangerous to humans. In fact, their venom is weaker than a bee's sting, and they're more likely to flee than attack. It turns out these creepy crawlers are more afraid of us than we are of them

693. "Star Wars: The Force Awakens" holds the record for the highest-grossing opening weekend in film history, with a global revenue of $528 millionThe highest-scoring soccer (football) game in history took place in 2002 between AS Adema and SO l'Emyrne in Madagascar, ending with a score of 149-0.

694. The first recorded instance of figure skating dates back to the 13th century in the Netherlands when people would skate on frozen canals using animal bones strapped to their feet.

695. The famous "Mona Lisa" painting by Leonardo da Vinci is only 30 inches tall by 21 inches wide.

696. The actor Christopher Walken worked as a lion tamer in a circus as a young man. He also has multicoloured eyes. One of them is blue and the other one is hazel brown—also referred to as heterochromia.

697. Pop star Taylor Swift has a fascination with the number 13.

698. Basketball, the beloved sport around the world, was invented by a Canadian PE teacher James Naismith, in 1891.

699. The famous painting "The Scream" by Edvard Munch has four versions.

700.   In 1963, Major League Baseball pitcher Gaylord Perry joked that a man would walk on the moon before he hit a home run.

701.   In the film "The Shawshank Redemption," the role of Tommy Williams, played by Gil Bellows, was initially offered to Brad Pitt, who turned it down.

702.   The first color to be synthesized chemically as a pigment was Egyptian blue.

703.   Andre the Giant played Bigfoot in the 1989 movie "Uncaged."

704.   The city of Portland was named by a coin flip.

705.   Rapid Eye Movement (REM) sleep typically begins 90 minutes after falling asleep.

706.   Madonna, also known as the Queen of Pop, is the female artist who has sold the most records throughout her career.

707.   The Hope Diamond is worth between $250 and $350 million.

708.   More than three million people visit the Tower of London each year to see the Crown Jewels, making it the country's top tourist destination.

709.   In the year 1802, the first game of Gaelic football was played in Ireland, and since then, it has evolved to become its most popular sport.

710.   Robert De Niro received two Academy Awards: one for best supporting actor in The Godfather, Part II and another for best actor in Raging Bull for his depiction of boxer Jake La Motta.

711. Students in the United States Navy's premier fighter pilot training school, known as TOPGUN, are given a $5 fine if they refer to the film Top Gun.

712. The original Leonardo da Vinci's "The Last Supper," created between 1495 and 1498, is one of the most iconic paintings in the world. Although there have been countless copies done in all sizes, the original masterpiece measures approximately 15 feet by 29 feet.

713. The inaugural Formula One Grand Prix in the Middle East was held in Bahrain in the year 2004.

714. The Dolphins were the first team in NFL history to finish a whole season unbeaten. Their 1972 season finished without a loss and culminated in a victory in Super Bowl VII.

715. Music legend Ray Charles began facing vision problems around the age of seven. Doctors believe that juvenile glaucoma was the cause of his blindness. However, Charles remained unphased, insisting that his visual impairment would not hold him back—he wasn't wrong!

716. People with hyperosmia are also called "super smellers". They possess an extraordinary and super heightened sense of smell compared to the average person!

717. Tsundoku is the Japanese word meaning the joy of possessing more books than you'll ever have time to read.

718.   While koalas may look cute and cuddly, they can be quite feisty when they feel threatened. Koalas have sharp teeth and claws that they won't hesitate to use in self-defense. So, while they might appear harmless, it's best to admire them from a distance.

719.   Boxing Day, celebrated the day after Christmas, has nothing to do with the sport of boxing! There seems to be a bit of confusion about this, but actually the term originated in the United Kingdom and traditionally involved employers presenting their workers with "Christmas boxes". These would often contain gifts, money, or bonuses. Today, it has evolved somewhat into a day of relaxation, sometimes shopping, and basically enjoying any leftovers from the previous day! Mince pie anyone?

720.   Unlike many animals, prairie voles form monogamous pair bonds and stay together for life. These tiny rodents demonstrate their affection through grooming, cuddling, and other adorable behaviors, proving that love can be found even in the most unexpected places.

721.   The first episode of Star Trek, "The Cage," featured Captain Pike rather than Captain Kirk. However, Spock was mentioned! NBC rejected the initial pilot of the show, but ordered a second, which introduced Kirk, Scotty, and Sulu.

722.   The Louvre is not only the museum with the highest number of annual visitors, but it is also the largest museum in the world. Many notable works of art are housed in the Louvre Museum, including Leonardo da Vinci's Mona Lisa and the Venus de Milo statue.

723. At the time of writing, Leonardo da Vinci's Salvator Mundi is the most expensive painting ever sold. The painting sold for 140 million dollars in 2017.

724. Elvis Presley, known as the "King of Rock and Roll", was also a talented actor and starred in 31 feature films during his career. His first movie, "Love Me Tender", premiered in 1956, and its title song became one of his biggest hits.

725. Nirvana, the legendary American rock band, was formed in 1987. The lead vocalist and guitarist for the band was, of course, Kurt Cobain. The band went through a series of drummers, the most notable being Dave Grohl who later went on to form the Foo Fighters.

726. Bill Murray apparently improvised most of his lines whilst playing his role as the groundskeeper in Caddyshack.

727. In Spain, football is by far the most popular sport, although basketball is a close second.

728. It would appear that the late Queen Elizabeth II enjoyed the works of Dr. Seuss! In the year 2000, the Queen attended the premiere of the film "How the Grinch Stole Christmas".

729. Elizabeth Montgomery, who played the witch Samantha in Bewitched, never wiggled her nose in real life despite the fact that she did so in the role. It was all down to a camera trick.

730. The late Queen Elizabeth II joined the Auxiliary Territorial Service (ATS) when she was just 19 years old. She trained as a driver and mechanic, earning the rank of Second Subaltern, which is the equivalent to second lieutenant.

731. Harry Houdini was born in Budapest, Hungary, in 1874. He was not only a famous illusionist and escape artist, but also an accomplished pilot. He became one of the first pilots to fly a plane in Australia. Houdini's passion for aviation was so strong that he even briefly considered giving up his magic career to focus on flying.

732. There is evidence suggesting that wrestling is among the world's oldest sports. The renowned cave paintings of Lascaux, France, which are estimated to be over 15,000 years old, depict scenes of wrestling.

733. The actor Christopher Walken received an MTV Video Music Award for choreographing his own dance routine in the music video "Weapon of Choice" for Fatboy Slim.

734. Babe Ruth, a legendary figure in the realm of baseball, gained widespread acclaim for his astonishing home run achievements. However, he also had a talent for pitching! Before becoming a full-time outfielder, Ruth played as a left-handed pitcher for the Boston Red Sox, accumulating an impressive win-loss record.

735.   The world's longest movie ever made is "The Cure for Insomnia," directed by John Henry Timmis IV. The film lasts for 85 hours and premiered in its entirety at The School of the Art Institute in Chicago, Illinois, from January 31 to February 3, 1987.

736.   The can-can was originally a dance for couples, and its wild and suggestive nature caused a scandal. It wasn't until the 1840s that it became the theatrical form familiar today, performed by a chorus line of female dancers with acrobatic agility.

737.   During the early 1900s, "marathoning" was a popular sport with events that went as far as 900 miles. These ultra-marathon pedestrian competitions were held in the United States, and the participants were often called pedestriennes.

738.   There is evidence from archaeological digs that show tobacco was used by the Mayan people of Central America around the first century BC. It is suggested that they smoked tobacco leaves as part of their religious and ceremonial rituals.

739.   Throwing an apple at someone you admired was considered a symbol of high respect in Ancient Greece.

740.   Joan of Arc left more than just an historical impact. In addition to freeing France, her cropped hair became known as the bob cut.

741.   When eating noodles in Japan, it is customary to slurp them. This is perfectly acceptable dinner table etiquette in Japan!

742. Vanilla ice-cream is probably the favourite for most people, but in Japan things are very different. In Tokyo's Namjatown indoor amusement park, there is a restaurant called "Ice Cream City" where you can try some of the strangest flavours imaginable and even some that would seem quite unpalatable. Yes, if you fancy an oyster or eel flavoured ice-cream, Japan is the place to go. Or how about a nice curry flavour ice-cream? I think I will stick to good old vanilla for now.

743. Mark Twain asserted that he was the first author to use a typewriter, and that he handed his publisher a typewritten copy of the whole manuscript for his book "Life on the Mississippi".

744. The "Park Playhouse", which opened in 1732, was the first theatre on Broadway.

745. Guinness, the renowned Irish beer, was created in 1759 in Dublin.

746. George Lucas originally aspired to be a race car driver. After a near-fatal vehicle accident, however, he changed his mind.

747. Avatar is still the most successful film of all time as of 2023. It was overtaken for a short period by "Avengers: Endgame" but with talk of Avatar 2 being made, the film made a comeback to the top spot.

748. Jamaican sprinter Usain Bolt, widely considered the fastest man in the world, holds the world record for the 100-metre sprint, with a time of 9.58 seconds.

749.   Did you know that the tie originated in Croatia? It began as a piece of cloth worn by Croatian mercenaries and was called a cravat, which is where we get the word "cravat" from.

750.   Salvador Dalí often used melted clocks in his paintings to symbolize the relative nature of time and the persistence of memory.

751.   The longest-running Broadway show is "The Phantom of the Opera," which opened in 1988 and has performed over 13,000 shows.

752.   The annual "Running of the Brides" in Bangkok, Thailand, sees hundreds of couples racing to get their hands on a free designer wedding dress.

753.   Every year, on February 2nd, the United States and Canada celebrate Groundhog Day. According to tradition, if a groundhog comes out of its burrow and sees its shadow, there will be six more weeks of winter. If it doesn't see its shadow, then spring is on the way!

754.   Oktoberfest in Munich, Germany, is the world's largest beer festival, drawing millions of visitors every year.

755.   There are over 700 different kinds of purebred dogs. The American Kennel Club recognizes 190 breeds, and new breeds are still being created and discovered.

756. The highest-grossing film of all time, as of my last update, is "Avatar," which reclaimed its title after a re-release in China.

757. Blue and white porcelain was popular throughout the Ming Dynasty, which was 1368 to 1644. Blue-glazed pottery and porcelain get their distinctive color from cobalt ores which were brought from Persia. At the time, cobalt was difficult to obtain and therefore costly and only used in small amounts.

758. The board game known as Monopoly can be traced back to the early part of the 20th century. The first known version of the game, which was given the name "The Landlord's Game" and was patented for the first time in 1904.

759. The small English village of Sonning-on-Thames erected a sign declaring itself the "Centre of the Universe." Among the village's notable residents is the renowned actor George Clooney.

760. The "Bollywood" name was coined during the 1970s, combining Bombay (the city now known as Mumbai) with Hollywood (the center of the United States film industry).

761. 'Elementary, my dear Watson,' is a phrase that the fictional character Holmes never actually said in any of Conan Doyle's original novels.

762. Despite his reputation as an English author, C. S. Lewis was actually Irish and was born in Belfast, Northern Ireland in 1898.

763.   Throughout his career, Michael Jackson donned a crystal-studded glove on stage and in music videos. Michael's accessory originally appeared on television in 1983.

764.   The world's longest-running animated television show is the comedy "The Simpsons," which is still very much in production!

765.   Before becoming an actor, Jason Statham was a member of the British National Diving Squad, culminating with his participation at the 1990 Commonwealth Games in Auckland, New Zealand.

766.   Rod Stewart's New Year's Eve performance at Copacabana Beach in Rio de Janeiro, Brazil, set the record for the highest attendance for a free concert event. Over 4 million people flocked to the beach to watch him perform! 4 million!

767.   The biro pen, the British word for a ballpoint pen, was named after its Hungarian creator and inventor, Laszlo Biro. Biro's invention was an overnight economic success, and he received the majority of the credit for the simple and elegant design.

768.   Pablo Picasso holds the record for the artist with the most stolen artworks, with over 1,000 of his paintings reported missing or stolen.

769.   The Cannes Film Festival is one of the most prestigious and publicized film festivals in the world. It has been held annually in Cannes, France, since 1946.

770.   In the world of fashion, Paris, Milan, New York, and London are known as the "Big Four" and host the most important fashion weeks.

771.   The first-ever "talkie," or movie with sound, was "The Jazz Singer," released in 1927. It revolutionized cinema and marked the decline of silent films.

772.   The original Olympic Games were held in ancient Greece every four years for over a thousand years until they were banned by Roman Emperor Theodosius I in AD 393.

773.   Ballet originated in the Italian Renaissance courts of the 15th century and was further developed in France and Russia as a concert dance form.

774.   Ludwig van Beethoven began to experience hearing loss in his late 20s and was almost completely deaf by his 40s.

775.   In Indiana Jones and the Raiders of the Lost Ark, the famous scene where Indiana Jones shoots a sword-wielding opponent was unplanned.

776.   The modern piano, invented around 1700, has evolved from Beethoven's piano which had only 79 keys to today's standard pianos which have 88 keys.

777.   Banksy's "Girl with Balloon" shredded itself after being sold at an auction in 2018.

778.   Aerosmith's lead singer, Steven Tyler, has another talent outside of music. He is also an accomplished artist. Tyler specializes in painting and had an exhibition of his artwork in 2018.

779.   Did you know that only five sports have been featured at every summer Olympic Games since 1896? These are fencing, swimming, cycling, gymnastics, and athletics.

780.   A signet ring is customarily worn on the little finger of the non-dominant hand. This practice has historical roots and is still observed today, as it allows for ease of use when imprinting the ring's unique engraving or seal into wax or other materials.

781.   In 1923, Mary Ellison, an American lady better known by her ring moniker "The Fabulous Moolah", became the first female professional wrestler.

782.   Chocolate has been adored by people around the world for centuries. Its creamy, sweet flavor has been loved since it was first introduced to Europe by Spanish conquistadors in the 16th century. The Mayans discovered cacao and would make a brew from the bitter bean, referring to this sweet beverage as "chocolhaa," which means hot water.

783.   In 1972, the chess champion Bobby Fischer requested that all cameras be removed from the playing hall during his World Chess Championship match against Boris Spassky. The match was halted due to Fischer's insistence, and it was only after the cameras were removed that the games resumed.

784.   The modern game of chess has been around for over 500 years. It is believed to have originated in India before spreading to Persia, the Islamic empire, and then to Southern Europe.

785.   "Born to Run" by Bruce Springsteen is widely regarded as one of the greatest rock albums of all time. Springsteen's third studio album, it was released on August 25, 1975, by Columbia Records. As his effort to break into the mainstream, the album was a commercial success and became his first to be featured on the Billboard 200 chart.

786.   Tim Burton is a notable director known for his unique gothic-fantasy style. He has worked on several successful films, such as "Edward Scissorhands," "The Nightmare Before Christmas," and "Alice in Wonderland."

787.   Audrey Hepburn's fashion style is timeless. She is particularly remembered for her little black dress designed by Hubert de Givenchy. The dress gained iconic status after Hepburn wore it in the film "Breakfast at Tiffany's."

788.   Salvador Dalí is known for his striking and bizarre images in his surrealist work. His best-known painting, The Persistence of Memory, was completed in August 1931 and is one of the most famous surrealist artworks.

789. The Mona Lisa, Leonardo da Vinci's masterpiece, is known for its unique mystique and enigmatic smile. It is currently housed in the Louvre Museum in Paris and holds the record for the highest known insurance valuation in history at $100 million in 1962, which is worth nearly $850 million in today's money.

ASTRONOMY

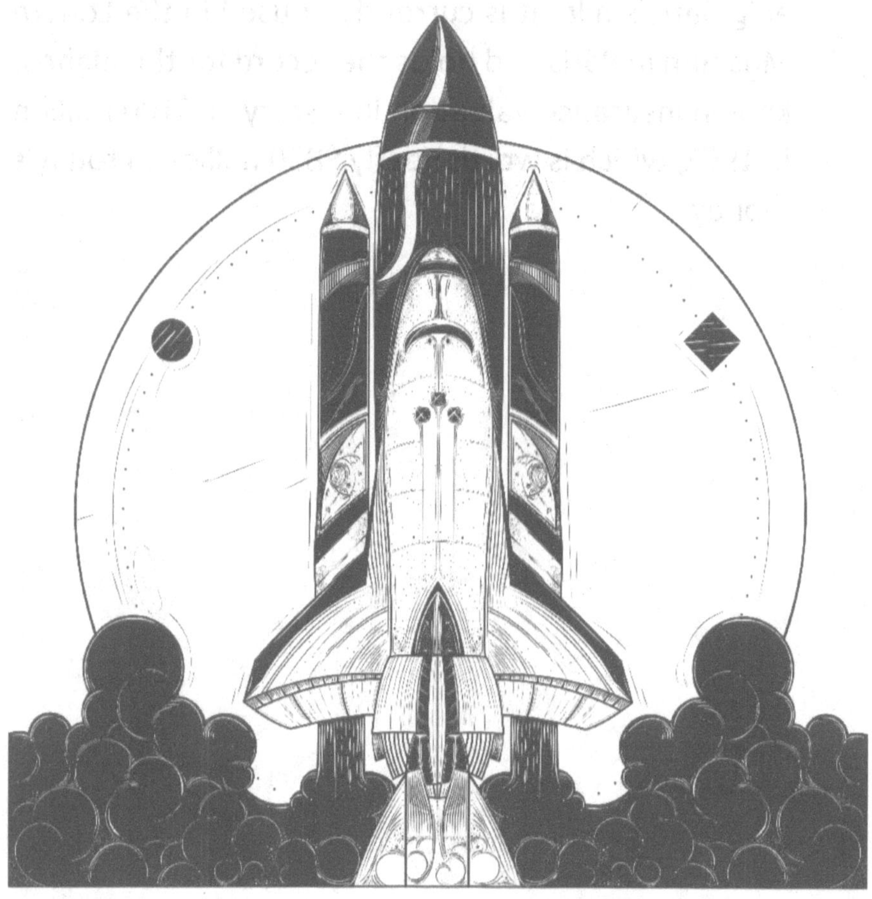

790. The Hubble Space Telescope (HST) was launched into orbit in 1990. The HST is named after the American astronomer Edwin Hubble, who is known for his discovery that the universe is expanding.

791. Venus, the second planet from the Sun, is often regarded as Earth's sister or twin planet due to its comparable size and similar characteristics

792. The surface of the Sun is called the photosphere. It has a temperature of about 5,500 degrees Celsius, which is hot enough to vaporise any known solid material.

793. Neil Armstrong retired from NASA in 1971 and spent the next decade teaching aeronautical engineering at the University of Cincinnati.

794. The Hubble Space Telescope orbits Earth at an altitude of around 340 miles and travels at a speed of 17,000 mph.

795. On average, the distance between Earth and the Moon is enough to fit 30 Earth-sized planets in a row.

796. On Mercury, a day is equivalent to 176 Earth days.

797. The Phoenix Lights, also known as "Lights Over Phoenix," were a string of UFO sightings reported over Arizona and Nevada on March 13, 1997.

798. The planet Saturn is well-known for its stunning rings. The rings are theorised to consist of ice, dust, fragments of comets, asteroids, and even bits of broken moons that were blasted apart by Saturn's strong gravity long before they reached the planet!

799. Neptune, the eighth and farthest planet from the sun in our solar system, experiences incredibly strong winds that can reach speeds of up to 1,300 miles per hour. That's almost nine times faster than the strongest winds ever recorded on Earth!

800. During a total solar eclipse the temperature can drop by as much as 10°C in just a few minutes!

801. Pluto is no longer classified as a planet, as its orbital path is populated by numerous asteroids and other types of space rocks; in contrast, the orbits of the larger planets in our solar system, or true planets, are clear of such space debris because they have been absorbed by the planets themselves over time. So, Pluto is really just one large space rock! In scientific terms, though, Pluto is still defined as a dwarf planet.

802. Astronomers estimate there are around 10,000 stars for every grain of sand on Earth, and that's just in the observable universe.

LAW, CRIME, PUNISHMENT, GOVERNMENT & POLITICS

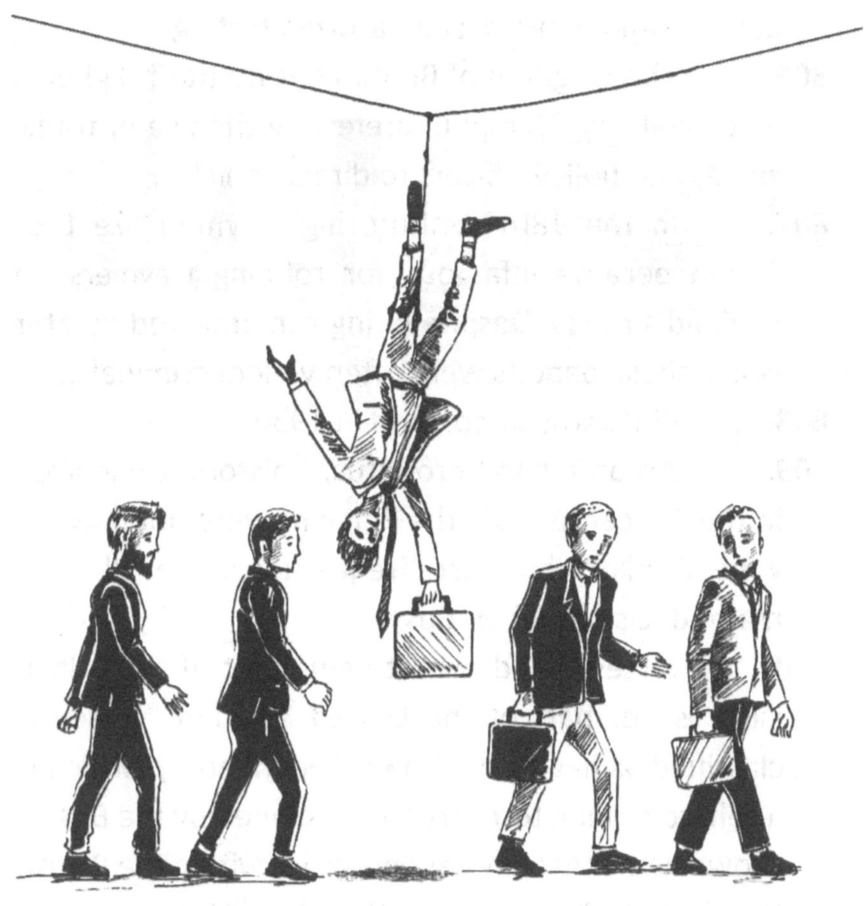

803. In medieval England, trial by ordeal was a practice where the accused was subjected to painful tasks, with the outcome believed to determine guilt or innocence through divine judgment.

804. Alcatraz Island, located in San Francisco Bay, was once home to a notorious federal prison known for housing infamous inmates like Al Capone.

805. Finland's education system is often hailed as one of the best in the world, with an emphasis on equality and minimal standardized testing.

806. The Kingdom of Bhutan has no traffic lights in its capital city, Thimphu, preferring the use of traffic circles and police officers to direct vehicles.

807. In the 18th century, highwaymen like Dick Turpin became infamous for robbing travelers on England's roads. Despite being romanticized in later years, these bandits were often violent criminals.

808. Pluto was discovered in 1930.

809. According to Herodotus, a historian who lived in the 5th century BC, the Persians were not only big wine drinkers but also frequently made all their major decisions when tipsy.

810. Jersey island, whilst being part of the British Isles, is not part of the United Kingdom. Jersey is classified as having a "Crown Dependency," which is a self-governing territory that is owned by the British Crown. Other Crown Dependencies within the British Isles include Guernsey and the Isle of Man.

FOOD & DRINKS

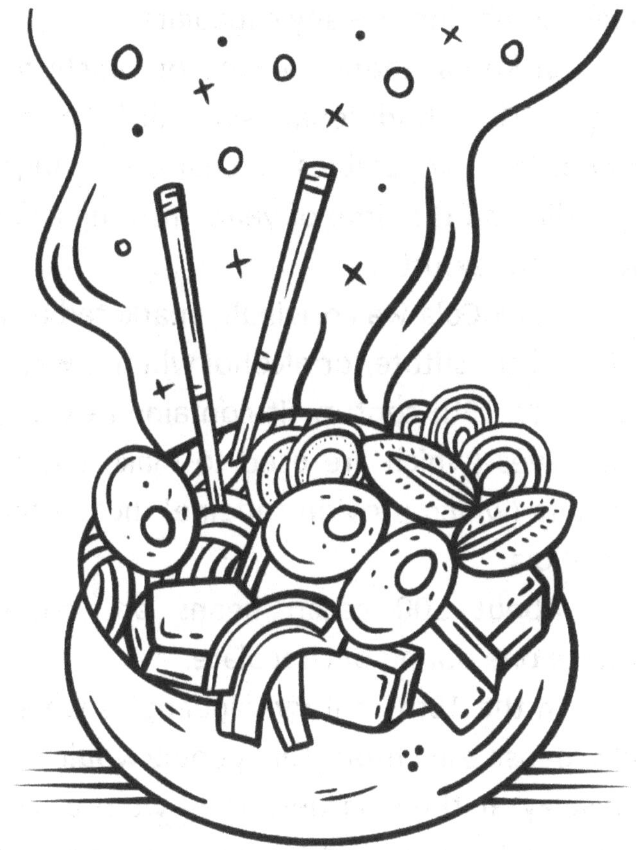

811. Escargot, a delicacy consisting of cooked land snails, is highly esteemed in French cuisine and has been eaten for thousands of years. They're usually served in their shells and prepared with garlic, butter, and parsley.

812. The first cookbook known and found was from Roman times and has a recipe for making jam! We're not quite sure of the flavor, though.

813. The first known recipe for brownies appeared in the 1897 Sears, Roebuck & Co. Catalogue, but the recipe did not include any chocolate.

814. In Korea, there's a type of kimchi for every season! This traditional side dish made from fermented vegetables changes ingredients depending on the time of year, ensuring a variety of flavors and textures.

815. Coca-Cola was originally marketed as a nerve tonic and substitute for alcohol when it was created in the late 19th century. It contained extracts from coca leaves (which are used to make cocaine) and kola nuts (which provide caffeine), hence the name "Coca-Cola."

816. About 500 cacao beans are required to produce one pound of chocolate.

817. In the 18th century, pineapples were so rare and expensive in Europe that people would rent them to display at their parties. They were a symbol of wealth and status, and having a pineapple at your event was a sign of prestige, even if it was just for show.

818. The Caesar salad was not named after Julius Caesar, but rather after its creator, Caesar Cardini, an Italian-American restaurateur who invented the dish in 1924.

819. The world's oldest known recipe is a 5,000-year-old Sumerian beer recipe, inscribed on a clay tablet.

820. The croissant, a popular pastry often associated with France, actually originated in Austria in the 17th century and was called a "kipferl" before it was adapted by French bakers.

821. In the late 1800s, Jewish immigrants from Russia and Poland brought the process of salmon smoking to London's east end. Because refrigeration was limited, they smoked salmon to preserve it, thus bringing us the smoked salmon we know and love today.

822. Black River Falls, Wisconsin is home to the biggest frying pan in the world!

823. Scampi, the plural of scampo in Italian, refers to breaded prawns or langoustine. In Britain, the term scampi strictly applies to langoustine; if it's not langoustine, it's not considered scampi.

824. Ambergris is a solid waxy material found in the gut of a sperm whale. It has been utilized to stabilize the scent in perfumes for thousands of years.

825. Iranian Beluga caviar is officially the costliest caviar in the world—a kilo will set you back around 20,000 dollars.

826. Margarine was originally created as an inexpensive alternative to butter for members of the French military. Napoleon III offered a prize for a cheap butter substitute, and the result was margarine!

827. There's a special day dedicated to the beloved kitchen staple, the egg. World Egg Day is celebrated every year on the second Friday in October.

828. A baker developed the renowned Twinkie in Illinois in the 1930s. The name was inspired by a billboard advertising "Twinkle Toe Shoes."

829. Many non-Japanese people confuse sashimi and sushi, yet the two foods are very much different. Sushi is often created with rice, vegetables and often seaweed. While raw fish is a common sushi component, many sushi meals feature cooked or smoked fish, and some contain no seafood at all. Sashimi, on the other hand, is always simply raw fish served on its own.

830. The actor James Cromwell became a vegan after starring in the movie Babe, in which he performed alongside a friendly pig. After spending so much time with the animal, James decided to give up eating any kind of animal product again.

831. The word "vodka" comes from the Russian word for "water," and it was originally distilled in Russia in the 14th century.

832. The traditional Christmas pudding was influenced by Roman Catholicism. Christmas puddings include 13 key ingredients to signify the 12 apostles, plus Christ.

833. The first pizza delivery is believed to have occurred in 1889. The pizza was Margherita, and it was delivered to Queen Margherita of Savoy.

834. The famous Oktoberfest beer festival held in Munich, Germany, attracts over six million visitors each year!

835. The cheese-rolling competition held annually in Gloucestershire, England, is a quirky and thrilling event where participants race down a steep hill chasing after a wheel of cheese. Injuries are common, but the tradition has persisted for centuries, showcasing the locals' love for cheese and adrenaline-fueled fun.

836. The habanero pepper is known for its heat, which can exceed 300,000 Scoville units. This chili is not only about spice; it also has a floral aroma and is used in some traditional Yucatecan dishes.

837. In Ethiopia, a traditional coffee ceremony involves roasting green coffee beans and preparing boiled coffee in a vessel called a jebena, often with the addition of spices like cardamom.

838. The world's oldest restaurant, Restaurante Botin, has been operating in Madrid, Spain, since 1725.

839. The town of Wigan in England, holds the annual "World Pie Eating Championships." Contestants competed to see who could eat a meat and potato pie the fastest.

HEALTH & MEDICINE

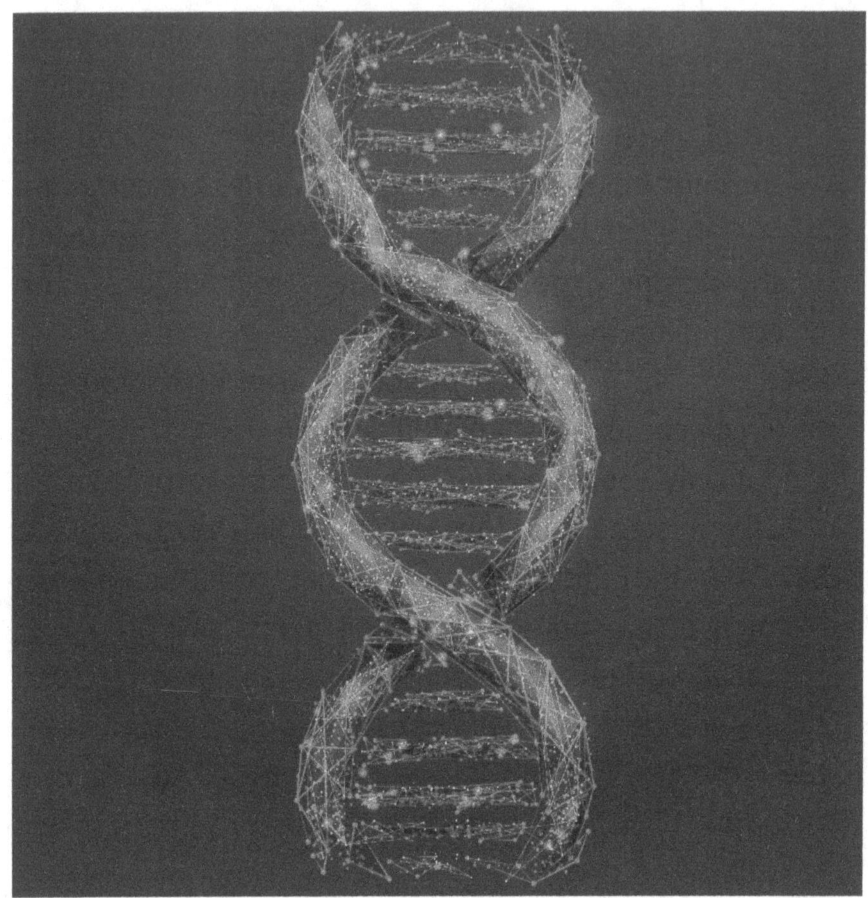

840. The human brain can process more information than the most powerful computer, but it still can't remember where you put your keys.

841. Insulin, a hormone that regulates blood sugar levels, is produced in the pancreas.

842. Myopia, or nearsightedness, is becoming increasingly common worldwide.

843. The human body produces heat as a result of metabolic processes. The average basal metabolic rate (the rate at which the body uses energy while at rest to keep vital functions going) can raise the temperature of a small room by a few degrees overnight.

844. Acupuncture is believed to have originated in China as far back as 100 BC.

845. Sleep stages include rapid eye movement (REM) and non-REM. There are three distinct phases of non-rapid eye movement (REM) sleep, including a light stage, a deep stage, and a dreaming stage. The average person will go through all four stages many times in a given night.

846. On July 21, 1983, the temperature at Vostok Station in Antarctica became the lowest ever recorded anywhere in the world.

847. At age 25, your brain has not yet finished developing.

848. An unhealthy dependence on cheese is possible.

849. The thighbone, or femur, is the longest and strongest bone in the human body.

850. Our bodies are veritable powerhouses, hosting over 600 skeletal muscles that make up roughly 40% of our body weight.

851. A taste bud has a short life lifetime—around 10 days!

852.   In 2015, Russian cosmonauts aboard the International Space Station (ISS) used leech therapy to treat a crew member's swollen leg.

853.   It has been proven in certain research that a person's stress levels may be lowered by being exposed to a specific aroma. The aroma of lavender, for instance, has been associated with reduced anxiety.

854.   It is possible for a king cobra, which is one of the most poisonous snakes in the world, to "stand up" and look a fully grown human being in the eye. When they are threatened, they are able to lift one-third of their body off the ground while simultaneously continuing to move forward to attack. King cobras are timid creatures that will, thankfully, stay away from humans whenever they can.

855.   The human body contains enough carbon to make approximately 9,000 pencils.

856.   The human nose can remember around 50,000 different scents.

857.   A person's sense of smell is a powerful memory and emotion trigger. This is because the region of your brain that processes odours (the olfactory bulb) is extremely near to the part of your brain that deals with emotion (the limbic system).

858.   Your skeleton is about as solid as concrete. That's not all that tough really if you think about what happens when you drop concrete on the floor—it tends to break!

859. Research suggests that the "guilty look" dogs display when they've done something wrong is more likely a reaction to their owner's angry or upset demeanor rather than an acknowledgment of guilt. Dogs are experts at reading human emotions and responding accordingly.

860. Leprosy is a chronic infectious disease caused by a slow-growing type of bacteria known as Mycobacterium leprae.

861. Andre the Giant had acromegaly, a disorder in which his body produces an excess of growth hormone, leading to his enormous stature.

862. Having heartburn during pregnancy is a common experience and it often occurs because of hormonal changes and the growing fetus pushing against the stomach.

863. Certain studies suggest that playing Tetris can help reduce the intensity of cravings for food, cigarettes, and alcohol by occupying parts of the brain used in imagery.

864. The term "quarantine" comes from the Italian "quaranta giorni," which means "40 days." This term originated during the 14th century when ships arriving in Venice from infected ports were required to sit at anchor for 40 days before landing.

865. Louis Pasteur developed the first vaccines for rabies and anthrax and is known for his contributions to the development of the first vaccine for chicken cholera.

866. The idea that the tongue is the strongest muscle in the human body is a commonly heard or read statement, but it's up for debate and depends on how one defines strength. If strength is measured by the ability to exert force, then the jaw muscle, also known as the masseter, takes the crown as the ultimate champion of strength. This muscle can exert an impressive 50 to 200 pounds of pressure, which is definitely enough to crack open a tough nut. I highly doubt the tongue could even come close to that kind of power.

867. According to studies, men with beards are more likely to be subconsciously perceived as having a higher social position.

868. A severe phobia of beards is known as pogonophobia. Pogon is derived from the Greek word for beards. A person with pogonophobia could experience intense fear or panic while around someone who has a beard! Gandalf from Lord of the Rings would be quite terrifying I would imagine.

869. Investigations of bacteria found that the average shower curtain can have up to 60 times more microbial life than a toilet seat.

870. Bees may not have a sense of smell for fear specifically, but they're actually quite adept at detecting the pheromones that are released when animals or humans become frightened. Their olfactory system allows them to collect scents and interpret their meaning. This means that they can sense perceived threats and react accordingly. While bees may not literally "smell" fear, they definitely have a finely tuned sense that helps them navigate their environment and stay safe from danger.

871. Gladiator sweat was considered an aphrodisiac. It is said that women would often mix it into skincare products.

RANDOM FACTS

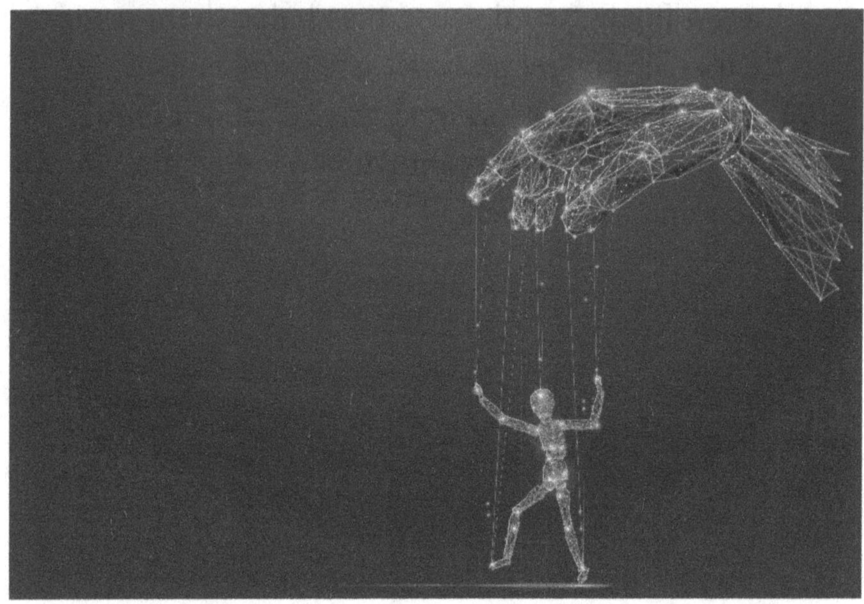

872. It takes more muscles to frown than it does to smile.

873. It takes 1,000 hours to master a new skill, according to the old saying "practice makes perfect."

874. "Buffalo buffalo Buffalo buffalo buffalo buffalo Buffalo buffalo" is a grammatically correct sentence in English.

875. In the United States, more people are allergic to cow's milk than any other food.

876. A lightning bolt can reach temperatures hotter than the surface of the sun!

877. It's illegal to pump your own gas in the U.S. states of New Jersey and Oregon

878. One of the most exclusive and expensive chess sets in the world is the Jewel Royale Chess Set, which is worth over $1 million.

879. Crayola crayons' most popular color, according to a survey, is blue.

880. LEGO was founded in 1932 by Ole Kirk Christiansen. The name LEGO is derived from the Danish words "leg godt," which means "play well".

881. The 45th parallel north is a circle of latitude that is exactly halfway between the Equator and the North Pole.

882. A baby octopus is roughly the size of a flea when it is born.

883. Ketchup was once sold as a medicine in the 1830s.

884. Pigeons were used as mail carriers during wars.

885. Human birth control pills work on gorillas.

886. Inflation has caused the Zimbabwean dollar to suffer so much that people were literally carrying around billions of Zimbabwean dollars which were worth only a few US dollars.

887.   Less than 10% of the world's currency is physical money, the rest is digital.

888.   "Borborygmus" is the noise that your stomach makes when you're hungry.

889.   You cannot snore and dream at the same time.

890.   The shortest war in history lasted 38 minutes, between Britain and Zanzibar on August 27, 1896.

891.   While it might seem like fingernails and hair continue to grow after death, this isn't the case. What actually happens is that the skin dries out and retracts, which can give the appearance of longer hair and nails.

892.   The word "checkmate" in chess comes from the Persian phrase "Shah Mat," which means "the king is helpless."

893.   Bubble wrap was originally designed to be used as wallpaper.

894.   The Empire State Building has its own zip code due to its size and the number of people working there.

895.   Harry Houdini, born Ehrich Weiss, took his stage name from the French magician Jean Eugène Robert-Houdin, who he initially admired.

896. The human tongue has around 10,000 taste buds, with each one containing up to 100 receptor cells for taste.

897. The term "blue blood" comes from the Spanish phrase "sangre azul," and is associated with the Spanish aristocracy who claimed purity of blood without Moorish or Jewish ancestry. Their veins appeared more prominently through their pale skin and thus looked blue.

898. The Mona Lisa, housed in the Louvre Museum, has no clearly visible eyebrows or eyelashes. Some art historians suggest this may be due to a restoration error.

899. Laughter is infectious; it can spread from one person to another even if they are just pretending to laugh.

900. More information is generated and transmitted by your neurons than by all of the phones in the world combined.

901. Greyhounds, known for their incredible speed, can reach up to 45 miles per hour in just a few seconds.

902. The number zero (0) was not introduced in Europe until the year 1200 AD, and it was brought there by Italian mathematician Leonardo Fibonacci, known for the famous Fibonacci sequence.

903. About 90% of the world's population lives in the Northern Hemisphere.

904. The strongest biological substance is spider silk.

905. In the United States, the most populated ZIP Code is 60629 in Chicago, with over 113,000 residents as of the last census count.

906. The concept of daylight saving time was first proposed by George Hudson in 1895 to extend evening daylight for leisure activities by shifting clocks an hour forward during the summer.

907. The phrase "selling like hotcakes" originated in the United States during the 19th century. Hotcakes at county fairs were often so popular that they sold out fast, prompting the metaphorical saying.

908. Laptops were invented by Adam Osborne in 1981. The first portable computer was called the Osborne 1.

909. The word "lunch" is actually a shortened form of "luncheon," which is derived from the older word "nuncheon," a term for a quick snack between meals that you can eat with your hands.

910. A group of frogs is called an "army," while a group of toads is referred to as a "knot."

911. A single spaghetti noodle is called "spaghetto."

912. The fear of being tickled by feathers is known as "pteronophobia."

913. The "@" symbol is called an "arroba" in Spanish and Portuguese, deriving from the Arabic word for "quarter" (ar-roub), which was historically used to refer to a unit of weight or volume.

914. "Hello" became a popular telephone greeting thanks to Thomas Edison; before that, people used to say "Ahoy" on the phone, following Alexander Graham Bell's suggestion.

915. The amount of force used in a typical bite is about 70 PSI (pounds per square inch), but a bite during a stressful situation can be much stronger.

916. A "jiffy" is actually a scientific term, referring to the time it takes for light to travel one centimeter in a vacuum, approximately 33.4 picoseconds.

917. The name "Bluetooth" for the wireless technology standard is derived from the 10th-century Scandinavian king Harald Bluetooth who united Danish tribes into a single kingdom. The technology was named as such because it was designed to unite devices in a similar way.

918. In medieval times, knights would get on their horses from the left side because they carried their swords on the left to prevent the weapon from getting in the way.

919.   October used to be the eighth month of the year in the Roman calendar, which is why it's named after "octo," meaning "eight" in Latin.

920.   The highest-altitude city with over 100,000 inhabitants is La Rinconada, Peru, which sits at 16,732 feet above sea level.

921.   Aluminum used to be more valuable than gold. It was so prized that Napoleon III of France's most distinguished guests were given aluminum cutlery, while others made do with mere gold.

922.   In the 17th century, dildos were often made from leather, ivory, or metal and were handcrafted to provide pleasure.

923.   The study of clocks and timekeeping is known as horology.

924.   The first speeding ticket was issued in Dayton, Ohio in 1904. The speed demon was going 12 miles per hour.

925.   A peck is an imperial and United States customary unit of volume, equivalent to two dry gallons or eight dry quarts or sixteen dry pints.

926.   A time capsule in Oglethorpe University in Atlanta, known as the "Crypt of Civilization," is not to be opened until the year 8113. It was sealed in 1940 with artifacts of the era intended to provide future civilizations with a snapshot of life in the early 20th century.

927.   The Harmonic Turbine Engine is an innovative engine design that uses a continuous combustion process, as opposed to the intermittent explosions in a conventional internal combustion engine, to generate power more efficiently and with fewer emissions.

928.   Vinyl records have been making a comeback in recent years. The annual sales of vinyl surpassed CDs for the first time since the 1980s in the United States in 2020.

929.   During the 16th century, fake beauty marks were used to cover smallpox scars or blemishes and became a fashionable trend among both men and women in the European aristocracy.

930.   The original Ferris wheel was designed by George Washington Gale Ferris Jr. for the 1893 World's Columbian Exposition in Chicago. It stood at a height of 264 feet (80 meters) and could accommodate up to 2,160 passengers.

931.   There is a "right to repair" movement which advocates for legislation to allow consumers the ability to repair and modify their own electronics, to combat the trend of "planned obsolescence" where devices are designed to have a limited lifespan.

932.   The taste of water can be subtly influenced by its mineral content, which varies depending on the local geography and sources of water supply.

933.   Throughout history, different cultures have practiced trepanation, the act of drilling or scraping a hole into the skull, for various medical reasons, including the release of pressure and spirits.

934.   The term "blue blood" originated from the Spanish expression "sangre azul," indicating noble birth or aristocracy. It was believed that the aristocracy had veins appearing bluer than those of commoners, due to their fair skin which was less likely to be tanned from labor in the sun.

935.   Rats are known for their survival skills and have been noted to thrive in urban environments, often being considered pests due to their adaptability and high reproduction rate.

936.   The "golden hour" in photography refers to the period shortly after sunrise or before sunset, where the light is softer and warmer, providing ideal lighting conditions for photographs.

937.   In maritime tradition, a ship's bell is an important tool for signaling, keeping time, and providing an alarm in cases of emergency.

938. Rubber duck races, where thousands of rubber ducks are released into a river, have become popular fundraising events around the world.

939. The infinity symbol (∞) was first used by the mathematician John Wallis in 1655 to represent the concept of infinity.

940. The "Great Emu War" was an actual event in 1932, where the Australian military was called in to manage the emu population in Western Australia. The birds proved surprisingly difficult to capture and control, resulting in a failed campaign.

941. A barrister in the UK must pass an exam in order to wear a wig made of horsehair; this tradition started in the 17th century.

942. In the English legal system, only barristers are traditionally permitted to speak in the higher courts. Solicitors, meanwhile, have rights of audience in lower courts but must pass an examination to be "Higher Courts Advocates" for the right to speak in higher courts.

943. Prior to being used for currency, bank notes were first used by the Chinese during the Tang dynasty, as temporary certificates of deposit issued to those who had deposited money or valuables at a treasury.

944. Sigmund Freud's famous couch was covered with Persian carpets and chenille pillows. The couch is now on display at the Freud Museum in London.

945. The Blue Ribbon Sports Company, which eventually became Nike, was founded in January 1964.

946. In the United Kingdom, it's illegal to handle a salmon in suspicious circumstances. This unusual law is part of the Salmon Act of 1986.

947. In 1945, the temperature in Tokyo rose to 79 degrees Fahrenheit, making it the hottest recorded temperature at that time of the year.

948. There are 24 time zones around the world.

949. "Duff" is a British naval term for a pudding that's been boiled or steamed in a cloth bag or bowl.

950. In medieval times, the word "boredom" did not exist in the English language. The concept was described as "tedium," which is Latin for weariness or boredom.

951. The term "hangry" is a colloquial expression denoting a state of anger caused by lack of food; hunger causing a negative change in emotional state.

952. The name "Bluetooth" is derived from the 10th-century king of Denmark, King Harald Bluetooth, who was known for uniting parts of

Denmark and Norway. Similarly, Bluetooth technology was created to unify various devices with wireless communication.

953. The fashion industry in the U.S. alone is valued at 1.2 trillion dollars. This huge amount is a reflection of the price tag on our vanity and desire to express ourselves through clothing.

954. The world's longest recorded chicken flight lasted for 13 seconds.

955. A "butt" is actually a traditional unit of volume that's used for wines and other alcoholic beverages. It's equal to two hogsheads, which is about 126 gallons or 477 liters.

956. The game of roulette is also known as "the Devil's Game" because the numbers on the roulette wheel add up to 666.

957. Two pizzas were the first goods purchased with Bitcoin. In May 2010, a programmer by the name of Laszlo Hanyecz exchanged 10,000 Bitcoins for two Papa John's pizzas. At the peak of Bitcoin's value, those pizzas would have been worth a fortune!

958. The fear of long words is ironically called "hippopotomonstrosesquippedaliophobia."

959. The term "honeymoon" is believed to have originated from the tradition of giving newlyweds a month's supply of mead, which is made from honey, to ensure happiness and fertility.

960. "Lucid" comes from the Latin word "lucidus," meaning "clear." A lucid dream is a dream during which the dreamer is aware that they are dreaming and may be able to exert some control over the dream characters, narrative, and environment.

961. The phrase "worth your weight in gold" has been around for a long time, and it's often used to describe someone's value in a metaphorical sense. If you were to take it literally, an average person weighing about 62 kg would be worth nearly 3 million dollars at current gold prices, which can vary.

962. A single strand of Spaghetti is called a "Spaghetto."

963. The Great Pyramids were originally covered in white limestone, which would reflect the sun's light and make them shine like a gem.

964. "Hedgehog's dilemma" is a metaphor about the challenges of human intimacy. It describes a situation in which a group of hedgehogs all seek to become close to one another in order to share heat during cold weather. They must remain apart, however, as they cannot avoid hurting one another with their sharp spines. Though they all share the intention of a close reciprocal relationship, this may not occur, for reasons they cannot avoid.

965. Redheads require more anesthesia during surgery, approximately 20% more than the average patient.

966. During World War II, metal was so scarce that the Oscars given out were made of painted plaster for three years.

967. In the 18th and 19th centuries, aluminum was more valuable than gold and silver in some places. Napoleon III, the Emperor of France, had a set of aluminum cutlery for his most distinguished guests.

968. The game of basketball was invented in 1891 by James Naismith, a Canadian physical educator, and the first game was played with a soccer ball and two peach baskets for hoops.

969. Pigeons have been trained by the U.S. Coast Guard to spot people lost at sea.

970. A "jiffy" is an actual unit of time. It refers to the time it takes light to travel one centimeter in a vacuum, approximately 33.4 picoseconds.

971. The term "avocado" derives from the Aztec word "ahuácatl," which means "testicle." It's thought to reference the shape of the fruit or its traditional use as an aphrodisiac.

972.　　It takes 2,700 liters of water to produce the cotton needed to make a single t-shirt, which is enough for one person to drink at least for 900 days.

973.　　"Sonder" is the realization that each random passerby is living a life as vivid and complex as your own.

974.　　The "door close" button in an elevator is often a placebo and does not actually speed up the process of the doors closing.

LANGUAGE

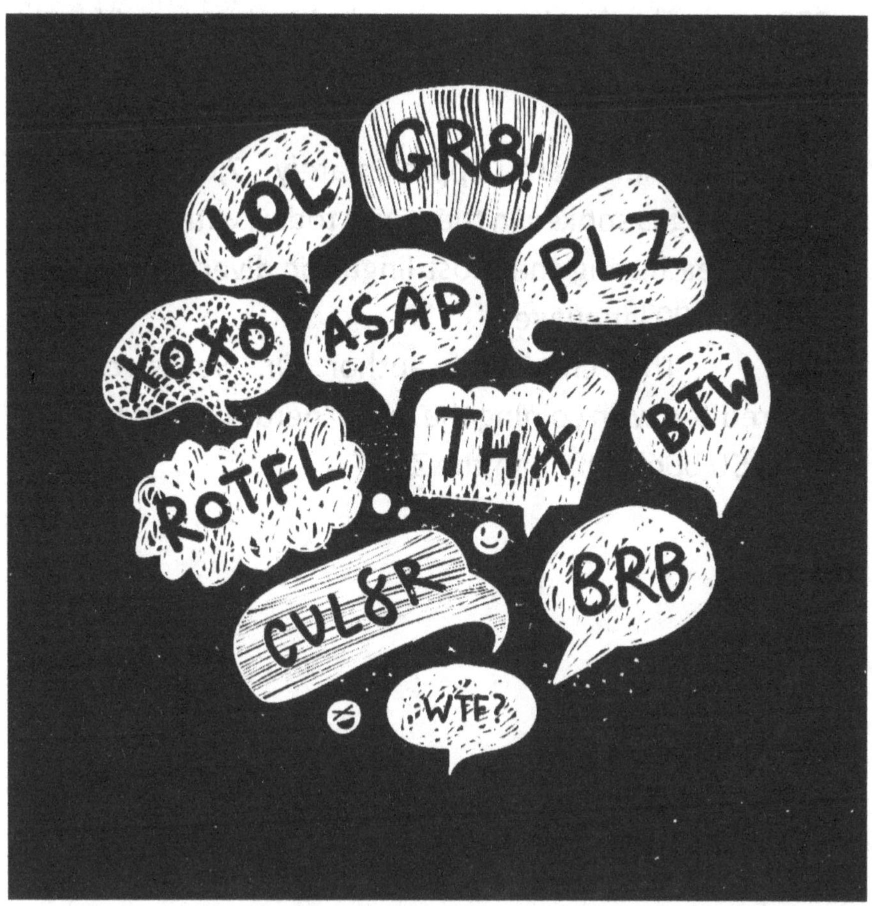

975. The most common letter in the English language is the letter 'E,' followed by 'A,' followed by the letter 'R.' It can be remembered by the word EAR. The least common letter is 'Z'.

976. Mohawk is an Iroquoian language spoken to this day by around 3,500 Mohawk people, who live mostly in Canada and to a smaller degree in the United States.

977. The Japanese language has three different writing systems: hiragana, katakana, and kanji.

978. The Turkish language holds the record for the longest word ever published in a dictionary. It has 70 letters.

979. There are approximately 7,000 different languages spoken in the world today, with Papua New Guinea having the most linguistic diversity, boasting over 800 languages!

980. The cherished author Dr. Seuss can be credited with coining the term "nerd" in his whimsical 1950 book, "If I Ran the Zoo."

MYTHOLOGY, HOLIDAYS, FOLKLORE AND CELEBRATION

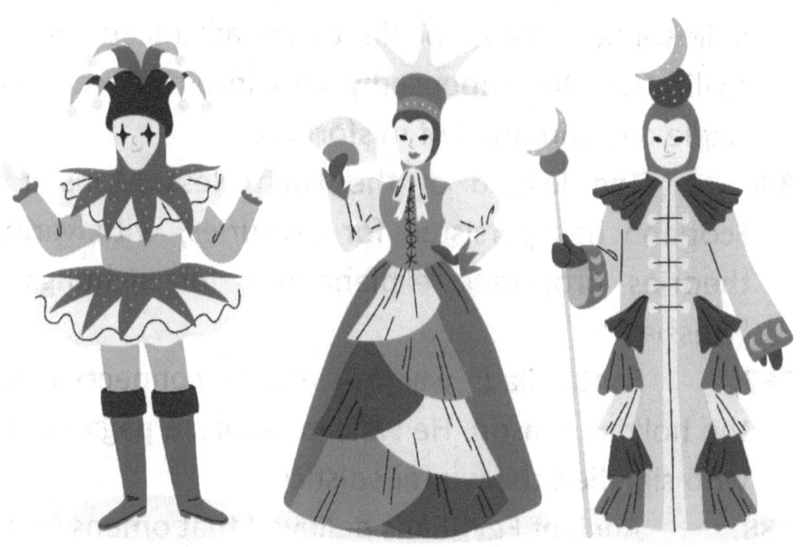

981. On the first Saturday in May, the United States celebrates National Homebrew Day, an event first proclaimed by Congress in 1988.

982. Holi, known as the Festival of Colors, is celebrated in India and Nepal by throwing colored powders, marking the arrival of spring and the victory of good over evil.

983. The Rio de Janeiro Carnival in Brazil is considered the biggest carnival in the world, with two million people per day on the streets celebrating with samba music and elaborate parades.

984. On April 12, 1961, Yuri's Night, also known as the "World Space Party," was established to celebrate Yuri Gagarin, the first human to journey into outer space and orbit the Earth on Vostok 1.

985. The myth of Atlantis, first described by the philosopher Plato, speaks of an advanced utopian civilization that supposedly sank into the ocean in a single day and night of misfortune.

986. The legend of the Loch Ness Monster in Scotland has persisted for centuries, with various theories proposing explanations for sightings of "Nessie."

987. Santa Claus was not always connected with the holiday season. He was, in reality, a pagan figure who signified the winter solstice.

988. Ancient Egyptians believed that omens of bad news might be detected in the sound or sight of an owl.

989. Some ancient cultures believed that placing coins on the eyes of the deceased would pay the toll for the afterlife's ferryman, Charon, in Greek mythology. This practice ensured safe passage for the soul to the other side.

990. In the 16th century, Queen Elizabeth I of England outlawed Christmas crackers because she considered they were too loud.

991. Folklore is also responsible for the history of the name "witch hazel." Native Americans and the first European settlers both made use of the witch hazel tree to locate underground water supplies. They would bring a divining rod with them, which consisted of a branch of witch hazel that had been bowed or crook, and they would use this as they traversed the land that they were surveying. They would watch the branch to see whether it bent or dipped because they felt that this indicated that they had located a source of water. This procedure was known as "water-witching," which ultimately led to the plant being used referred to as witch hazel in common parlance.

992.   The Japanese festival of Tanabata, based on a Chinese legend, is celebrated by writing wishes on small pieces of paper and hanging them on bamboo trees.

993.   The Norse mythology consists of nine worlds that are all connected by Yggdrasil, the world tree, which is an immense ash tree considered very holy.

994.   Saturnalia was an ancient Roman festival in honor of the deity Saturn, held on December 17th and later expanded with festivities through to December 23rd. The holiday was celebrated with a sacrifice at the Temple of Saturn, a public banquet, followed by private gift-giving, continual partying, and a carnival atmosphere.

995.   In Greek mythology, the phoenix is a long-lived bird that cyclically regenerates or is otherwise born again. Associated with the sun, a phoenix

obtains new life by arising from the ashes of its predecessor.

996. The Midsummer is celebrated in various forms across Europe, particularly in Nordic countries, where it is considered one of the most important holidays of the year, comparable only to Christmas and Easter in significance.

997. In Mexican culture, the Day of the Dead, or Día de los Muertos, is a celebration that takes place on November 1st and 2nd to honor and remember deceased loved ones, symbolizing the dead's spiritual journey.

998. The Chinese Moon Festival, also known as the Mid-Autumn Festival, is celebrated when the moon is believed to be the fullest and brightest, and it's a time for family reunions. Mooncakes, a rich pastry typically filled with sweet-bean or lotus-seed paste, are traditionally eaten during the festival.

999. According to Hindu mythology, Lakshmi, the goddess of wealth and prosperity, visits her devotees and bestows gifts and blessings upon them on Diwali, the festival of lights.

1000. In Celtic mythology, Samhain is a festival marking the end of the harvest season and the beginning of winter or the "darker half" of the year. It is celebrated from sunset on October 31 to sunset on November 1.

1001. The Krampus is a horned, anthropomorphic figure in Central and Eastern Alpine folklore, who during the Christmas season, punishes children who have misbehaved, in contrast with Saint Nicholas, who rewards well-behaved ones with gifts.

THE END

🚀 **Blast Off to Your Next Adventure!**

And that's a wrap, friends! We've zoomed past starry facts about space, tiptoed through tales of the animal kingdom, and unraveled mysteries of our amazing world, all with the turn of a page. We hope these facts have tickled your brain and that your appetite for knowledge has grown bigger with every fun fact you've discovered.

Remember, every day is a chance to learn something new, so keep this book close for your next curious quest. Whether you're at home, at school, or on a road trip, let this collection of wonders be your guide to endless exploration.

Before you close the cover and run off on your next adventure, we've got a tiny request. If this book made you smile, think, or say "wow," we'd be over the moon if you'd take a moment to drop a review on Amazon. Your thoughts mean the world to authors like us and help other curious minds find their way to fun learning just like you did.

Until next time, keep questioning, keep exploring, and keep that curiosity alive! Thank you for journeying with us through the pages of this book. Now, go on and share the

wonders you've learned—you're a fact-finder
extraordinaire!

**Happy discovering, and don't forget that Amazon
review!**